The 20 British Prime Ministers
of the 20th century

Campbell-Bannerman

ROY HATTERSLEY

HAUS PUBLISHING • LONDON

First published in Great Britain in 2006 by
Haus Publishing Limited
26 Cadogan Court
Draycott Avenue
London SW3 3BX

www.hauspublishing.co.uk

A CIP catalogue record for this book is available from the British Library

ISBN 1-904950-56-6

Designed by BrillDesign
Typeset in Garamond 3 by MacGuru Ltd
info@macguru.org.uk

Printed and bound by Graphicom, Vicenza

Front cover: John Holder

Contents

Introduction

For most of the 20th century, Henry Campbell-Bannerman was remembered – if he was remembered at all – as no more than the only Prime Minister to die in Downing Street. He was the tenant of Number 10 for less than three years and, in consequence, befell the fate which prejudices our judgement when we think of Rosebery, Bonar Law and Douglas-Home. We automatically assume, with more justification in their case than in his, that so brief a tenure cannot have produced much of lasting value. That assumption has become received wisdom. We believe that a fleeting tenure confirms, beyond doubt, that the brief incumbent had neither personal nor political importance. In fact, Henry Campbell-Bannerman was a politician of substance whose achievements changed the course of British history.

John Morley, Gladstone's biographer as well as his loyal political lieutenant, wrote, in what was generally a panegyric, that Campbell-Bannerman lacked the 'shining ... qualities which marked the last five holders of his Great Office' – Balfour, Salisbury, Rosebery, Gladstone himself and Disraeli. If 'shining' means the dazzling light of glamour, he was right. At a banquet given by Edward VII for the Prime Ministers of the Empire, a lady asked the premier of Canada who was 'that pleasant looking gentleman who is enjoying his dinner so much?' That, she was told, 'is your Prime Minister'.

But all that glisters is not gold and Campbell-Bannerman explicitly and continually avoided the sort of publicity which would have made him a personality. That does not mean that he was not harmed by the comparison with more glamorous and publicity-minded Prime Ministers – both the five who preceded him and Asquith and Lloyd George who followed. But it does not diminish the achievements of his premiership.

The greatest among them was the introduction of a basic (state-managed and funded) old age pension. Asquith and Lloyd George got the credit. But the genesis was slightly different from the myth. Henry Campbell-Bannerman resigned the office of Prime Minister on 3 April 1908. The names of the new Cabinet were published on 13 April. The announcement that Budget Day would be 3 May had already been made and it was thought that the maintenance of public confidence required that date to be honoured. Asquith toyed with the idea of remaining Chancellor of the Exchequer as well as being Prime Minister. Indeed when the King asked if the two jobs were not too much for one man, he argued that Gladstone had managed it – before he realised that times had changed and Gladstone was a phenomenon. He then decided to hand the Treasury to Lloyd George but make the budget speech himself. Subsequently, when problems arose about raising the revenue to pay for the old age pension after March 1909, the new Chancellor was happy to make clear that he was not responsible for the financial provisions – although he was happy to take credit for the scheme which they made possible. The fact is that change was made, albeit reluctantly, by Asquith, the Chancellor of the Exchequer when the new policy was adopted. Henry Campbell-Bannerman, the Prime Minister, supported the proposal with genuine enthusiasm. It was in his Cabinet that the fateful decision was taken.

The evidence that Campbell-Bannerman was more enthusiastic for the idea than Asquith is conclusive. In the budgets of 1906 and 1907, the Chancellor had steadfastly refused to advance into 'the stark uncharted territory of social reform'. Then the Liberal Party suffered unexpected defeats in two by-elections. The Labour candidate won Jarrow and in the Colne Valley – regarded as a stronghold of Liberal Nonconformity – Victor Grayson, a romantic and mysterious independent socialist, enjoyed an even more unlikely triumph. The government's insecurity increased when the TUC Annual Conference in Bath was unanimous in its support for the introduction of an old age pension on 1 January 1909.

The changes which have come to be called 'the beginning of the welfare state' had their origins in political necessity as much as in altruism. But reform – even when encouraged by a government's self-interest – is more likely to make rapid progress if it is consistent with the political instincts of the ministers who realise that life must move on. Asquith was not a radical. Campbell-Bannerman was. Everything we know about him – from his first unsuccessful by-election contest to his conduct as Prime Minister in the weeks before his death – confirms his genuine enthusiasm for reform.

The Parliamentary Labour Party – created in the slipstream of the 1906 Liberal landslide – expected the new government to introduce legislation to free trade unions from the burden of the Taff Vale Judgement, the court ruling which had made trade unions corporately responsible for damages incurred by their individual members during the course of a trade dispute. When the anticipated bill was not presented, as the Labour members hoped, by John Burns, the new Minister of Labour and the first genuine working man to sit in a British Cabinet, Walter Hudson, speaking on behalf of the Parliamentary Labour Party, attempted to change the law by private members' legislation. Campbell-Bannerman was so impressed with Hudson's argument that, without consulting colleagues, he promised to amend the Finance Bill to accommodate their demands. Asquith, on the contrary, thought it necessary to make a personal statement to the Committee of the Whole House, expressing his doubts about the change in government policy. There can be little doubt about the different ways in which the two men received the news that the Bath Conference of the TUC had demanded the introduction of an old age pension. Asquith thought the government had little choice but to take some sort of action. Campbell-Bannerman thought that the TUC demands were just.

Campbell-Bannerman's natural inclination shone through again in his relations with the suffragist movement – at best an irritant and at worst a danger – from the day on which he took office. Offended by the absence from the King's Speech of even a mention of extending the franchise, they demanded a meeting with the Prime Minister. When he refused, demonstrators managed to get inside both the official residence and official motor car. Wisely, Campbell-Bannerman forbade prosecution on the grounds that the women were *seeking notoriety and would be successful if they appeared before a magistrate.* Because of the suffragists' persistence he again, as in the case of the dissatisfied trade unionists, agreed to discuss the unresolved grievance with a delegation. Once again, he was too open-minded for the government's good. After a meeting which was more an harangue than a discussion, he told the women, *You have made before the country a conclusive and irresistible case.* But he added that, in present circumstances, there was no hope of legislation. The 'circumstances' were in the Cabinet. Campbell-Bannerman led a patrician administration to most of whom 'votes for women' was anathema.

It was not only his natural radicalism which made

Campbell-Bannerman respond to the demands of the Labour Party and express his sympathy with the claims of the suffragists. Nor was it the craven hope of political popularity. The evidence of his whole political career confirms that he was dangerously susceptible to rational argument. That weakness confounded him again after the Lord Chamberlain's refusal to licence the production of Bernard Shaw's 'The Shewing-up of Blanco Posnet'. Once again he agreed to meet the aggrieved parties and, once again, he began the meeting with an open mind. Once again he was convinced that the complainants' cause might at least be just. The group of distinguished writers argued eloquently that the ban was 'opposed to the spirit of the constitution, contrary to common justice and at variance with common sense'. The result was the Prime Minister's agreement to set up a Joint Committee of Both Houses to 'inquire into the censorship of stage plays as constituted by the Theatre Act of 1843'.

There are two ways of interpreting such intellectual flexibility. One attributes the changes of mind to infirmity of purpose – lack of confidence, clear principle and consistent purpose. The alternative explanation comes to the diametrically-opposed conclusion. It is built on the belief that rigidity is a weakness and willingness to be convinced a sign of strength. Henry Campbell-Bannerman's whole life confirms that the explanation of his conduct comes firmly within the second view. Equally important, despite the critics' claim that he was 'a plain unvarnished man, large of frame and soft of voice, short of opinion, honest and imaginative', he was reckless in his support for the great ideals in which he believed.

When steel was needed, steel he clearly demonstrated. As Secretary for War he stood up to Queen Victoria in his determination to remove her cousin, the ageing Duke of

Cambridge, from his long-held appointment as Commander-in-Chief of the Army. And, had he not resisted the pressure of his plotting colleagues who wanted Asquith to take his place, he would never have become Prime Minister. Most important of all in terms of character, he, almost alone among the Liberal leadership, was critical of the way in which the Boer War was fought. He even went as far as to commit the ultimate crime of politicians in time of war: he criticised the conduct of British soldiers under fire. But the brave speech which denounced the *methods of barbarism* which was herding women and children into camps and leaving them to starve was not his defining statement.

The essential Henry Campbell-Bannerman – practical, brave, determined and radical – was revealed during an early debate in the new Parliament of 1906. Arthur Balfour, the recently-defeated Tory leader, returned to Parliament in a contrived by-election, attempted to win over the House with an exhibition of elegant wit and contrived classical reflections – a technique which had made him the darling of the late Victorian Tory benches. In two dismissive sentences the new Prime Minister destroyed him. *Enough of this tomfoolery. It might have answered very well in the last Parliament, but it is altogether out of place in this ...*

Part One

THE LIFE

Chapter 1: 'Out of a Tory Nest'

Henry Campbell-Bannerman was born, plain but not simple, Henry Campbell in 1836. He was the second son of a prosperous, self-made merchant whose company – a partnership with his brother – imported raw material and exported finished goods, sold wholesale and retail drapery and acted as warehousemen for other businesses in Glasgow. The Campbells' fortune steadily increased. Henry was born in Kelvinside, a house which his father regularly rented for the summer. His real home was 129 Bath Street, which his father had built in the heart of Glasgow's 19th century redevelopment. But when he was 11, the family acquired the Strathcathro Estate in what was then called Forfarshire and is now Angus. The Campbells had become gentrified.

Just before the move to the country, Henry was enrolled in Glasgow High School – a year ahead of James Bryce who, like him, was to serve in future Liberal Cabinets. He stayed at the school for five years and then set out with his brother, James – his senior by more than ten years – on what amounted to a Grand Tour, even though their father hoped that they would pick up business along the way. On his return to Scotland – still not quite 16 – he registered to read Classics at Glasgow University. Although he won the gold medal for Greek, he did not sit the final examination. Campbell had more distinguished fish to fry. He became a Gentleman Commoner of

Trinity College, Cambridge, and graduated with a third class honours degree. He returned to Glasgow to work for J and W Campbell and thus qualified to become the first Prime Minister of Britain who could legitimately claim to possess commercial experience. But for Henry Campbell life on the shop floor was neither arduous nor long.

In 1860, at the age of 24, he became a full partner in his father's firm. It was, for Henry Campbell, an eventful year. While staying with his brother, he met Charlotte Bruce – a friend of his sister-in-law. After only one more meeting they became officially engaged – he 25 and she 28. It was a marriage of true minds. The partners, who often spoke to each other in French, shared a love of travel. And the sense of companionship increased with the years in which it seemed that they did everything together. When the great moment came for Henry to lead the Liberals into the election which resulted in that party's greatest landslide victory, there were some enthusiasts for Herbert Henry Asquith who argued that Campbell-Bannerman, as he had then become, was not well enough to accept responsibly the onerous obligations. The putative Prime Minister himself was only concerned about the possibility that his wife's health – never robust – would not allow her to survive the rigours of life in Downing Street.

At or about the time of his marriage, Henry Campbell-Bannerman became a Liberal. Nobody is very sure how or why. Augustine Birrell, another contemporary politician, wrote 'How CB became a Liberal I never knew. Certainly not by prayer, fasting or a course of hard reading'.[1] The most commonly-expressed explanations are that he was influenced either by his uncle or by Daniel Lawson, a rare radical among his father's 200 clerks. Henry's father was a Presbyterian and High Tory. But William Campbell had become a member of the Free Church and the Liberal Party. And it is at least possible that Birrell did Henry Bannerman less than justice. Shortly after his marriage, he sent Charlotte's brother (an Indian civil servant who had become chief of police in the state of Oudh) a copy of John Stuart Mill's *On Liberty*. Whatever the reason for his conversion from the faith of his fathers, in 1865 he was invited to stand as a Liberal candidate in Glasgow. He was not sure if he possessed the political vocation

'How CB became a Liberal I never knew. Certainly not by prayer, fasting or a course of hard reading'.

AUGUSTINE BIRRELL

and equivocated for so long that another, more enthusiastic candidate was found. But Colonel Bruce in India, no doubt benefiting from reading Mill, wrote to rejoice that Henry's thoughts had 'turned in the proper direction ... The sooner you get into parliament the better'.[2]

In April 1868 there was a by-election in the Stirling Burghs — a far-flung constituency which included Stirling itself, the port of Inverkeithing, Culdross, Dunfermline and the fishing village of Cowesferry. The vacancy arose when Laurence Oliphant was converted from Liberalism to spiritualism and left Westminster for a farm on Lake Erie in Michigan where he could follow his faith without inhibition. Henry Campbell was nominated as a 'radical Liberal'. And he more than justified the description. His election manifesto proclaimed that he supported household suffrage, the secret ballot, national and compulsory education, the disestablishment of both the Scottish and Irish churches and the end of primogeniture. He spoke to his electors about what he called his 'close connection' with James Campbell — by then a knight baronet. 'Through good report and through evil report, in fair weather and in foul, he has stuck to his party and his principles. So, in like manner, his son will stick to his.'[3]

No Tory stood in the contest. The Conservatives' choice of

candidate could not secure the necessary number of sponsors. So the by-election was between two Liberals, Whig and Radical. Despite Campbell's declared policy, his opponent – relying more on Henry's association than on his avowed beliefs – denounced him as a Tory in disguise. The local newspaper understood him better. It called him a 'spruce, well-groomed radical out of a Tory nest'. The electors of Stirling Burghs – being more interested in the nest than in the cuckoo – chose his opponent as their Member of Parliament.

He did not have to wait long. In the autumn of the same year, the Member for the Stirling Burghs had to fight the seat again in a general election. Campbell chose a local man as his agent and made unashamedly populist speeches. The majority of 71 won by his springtime opponent was over-turned into a majority of 519 for him. He remembered, when 33 years later he had become one of the great figures of the Liberal Party, that, from the start, he had never enjoyed dis-charging the tasks which a Member of Parliament is required to perform. He found *desperately little novelty in his constituency*. That notwithstanding, he remained happily united with the Stirling Burghs for almost 40 years.

The new Member of Parliament bought a house in Queen's Gate, a not very fashionable London district which the Forsytes regarded as 'the wrong side of the park'. The Campbells lived well. He regarded himself as a man of moderate tastes but his favourite meal was still *mutton broth, fresh herring or salmon, haggis, roast mutton or grouse, apple tart or strawberries*. He lived in London for five months of the year and Scotland during the summer when Parliament was not sitting. But he made regular visits to Paris and to Marienbad, a spa which he favoured because its physicians provided 'cures' for his chronic heart disease. Over the years he moved on to more fashionable districts and bigger houses – first to Eaton Square and then to

Grosvenor Place. Then he bought a country house at Meigle in Perthshire where they spent the high summers. They entertained, but not on the scale of the Asquiths and the Roseberys and would have done more had it not been for his wife's poor health. He was, in every particular, the epitome of upper-middle class propriety – as demonstrated by his strictures on the subject of Charles Stewart Parnell's adultery. *Parnell, by his conduct, [has] made it absolutely necessary that he should disappear from the face of public life.*[4] Even the conspicuously upright Mr Gladstone went no further than to mimic an Aberdeenshire crofter 'It'll na dae ...'. In fact, he was the quintessential middle-class radical and, once in Parliament, he demonstrated his progressive instincts by proposing that attendance at the schools envisaged in the anticipated Education Act should be compulsory. When the Bill was presented to Parliament, it included Campbell's suggestion.

For three years he devoted much of his time and energy to questions affecting Scotland. During earnest discussion, led by John Stuart Mill, about the iniquities of paying an official allowance to the soon-to-be-married Princess Louise, Campbell suggested that since the Queen's daughter was marrying the Scottish Marquis of Lorne, the increase in the Civil List would

The political philosopher John Stuart Mill (1806–73) developed and expanded upon the utilitarian philosophy of Jeremy Bentham and the thought of Adam Smith and David Ricardo, emphasising the vital role played by individual thought and action. In *On Liberty* and *The Subjection of Women* he championed such progressive causes as the emancipation of women, proportional representation, the development of farm collectives and the organisation of labour, forseeing many of the issues that were to emerge in the modern industrialised world. In 1865 he entered Parliament as MP for Westminster, serving until 1868.

at least result in more London money being transferred north of the border. The solemn John Stuart Mill was not amused. That uncharacteristic moment of flippancy is one of the few recorded humorous incidents in Henry Campbell's parliamentary life. The other oft-repeated anecdote – more popular with his enemies than with his friends – was originally reported by a Dunfermline journalist who noted that the Member for Stirling Burghs was a man whom 'Mr Gladstone passed in the lobby as if he were a stranger'. Anybody who remembered his first attempt at election took it for granted that the man who had introduced him at the hustings had described him as a future Prime Minister only because he was carried away by the excitement of the moment.

But preferment was not far away. And, immediately after it arrived, his personal fortunes improved at a speed that certainly matched, and probably overtook, the pace of his political progress. A wealthy uncle – Henry Bannerman – left Henry Campbell a life interest in Gennings, a massive estate of farms and farm cottages in Kent. There was, however, an onerous provision. The beneficiary was required to adopt the 'name of Bannerman either alone or in addition to his usual surname, but so that Bannerman shall be the last and principal name'. Charlotte urged him not to agree. And Henry himself had doubts about the metamorphosis. But in the end the attraction of the estate was too much to resist. He inherited the estate, moved in to one of the largest of his houses and became, at least officially, Henry Campbell-Bannerman. His wife continued to sign herself Charlotte Campbell and the recently hyphenated Member of Parliament only accepted his new name with bad grace. As late as 1884, 13 years after the addition, he was still apologising for his *horrid long name*, explaining that he was *always pleased to be called Campbell tout court*[5] and suggesting that a more convenient alternative, to which he was pleased to answer, was 'CB'. So CB he became and CB he remained for the rest of his life.

The inheritance was not the only piece of good fortune with which CB was blessed in 1871. In that year, he also joined the government as Financial Secretary to the War Office. Promotion to front from back bench is always a great occasion in the life of a young MP. Whether or not it is an augury of great things to come depends on more than the ability and industry of the new junior minister. The nature of the ministry, and its attraction to the new incumbent, often determines the success with which he accomplishes his duties.

Campbell-Bannerman was lucky. He was appointed to a job for which he felt immediate and instinctive enthusiasm. At the time of his appointment, his only association with military affairs had been a brief captaincy in the 1st Lanarkshire Volunteers. The company which he commanded was made up of men from his father's business. But, as the *Manchester Guardian* wrote, 'Mr Campbell-Bannerman fell in love with the war office ... it was characteristic of his Scottish fidelity of temperament that he stuck to it through good and evil report'.

His good fortune went further than an infatuation with his department. The Secretary of State for War was Edward Cardwell and he was embarking on the most radical programme of reform that the British army had ever faced. By the time that Campbell-Bannerman joined him at the War Office, some of the changes had already been accomplished. Small units had been withdrawn from the colonies, breech-loading rifles had become standard issue, flogging (a regular punishment for 'other ranks') was prohibited and short-term engagements (part with the colours and part with the reserve) were introduced to improve the quality of recruits. Politically, at least, most important of all, the purchase of commissions and promotion – often carried out at an auction room in Great Charles Street – had been abolished. Together with the opening up of the ancient universities to Dissenters and the recruitment of civil servants after examination rather than by patronage, the abolition of commission by purchase marked the beginning – intended by Gladstone's government if not by Gladstone himself – of the new age. Campbell-Bannerman became part of that march into the future.

However, other proposed reforms had yet to be completed. That, in its way, was also to Campbell-Bannerman's advantage. For it meant that for the next 30 years – in both government and opposition – there was still radical work for him to do. The modernisation of the artillery – still using muzzle-loading guns in 1871 – was one of the easier tasks facing the Secretary of State for War. Breaking the stranglehold of the Duke of Cambridge (cousin to Queen Victoria and Commander-in-Chief of the Army) was much more difficult. It was not accomplished until 'CB' himself was Secretary of State.

The job of Financial Secretary to the War Office was more of a test of Campbell-Bannerman's administrative skills than of his political flare. Cardwell had brought all the War Office together in one building on the south side of Pall Mall and had divided its work into three distinct departments – Military, under the Commander-in-Chief down the road in Horseguards, Supply under a Surveyor-General and Finance under the Financial Secretary. The task was made additionally exacting by the traditional Gladstonian view (heartily supported by Robert Lowe, the Chancellor) that the army should be reformed without incurring extra expenditure. Working in parallel with the Civil Service did nothing to convince CB of its willingness to absorb and implement new ideas. His proposals for a new method of accounting were sent to Cardwell with a covering note. *I have written this paper for your own reading only and have felt all the more free on that account. Had I taken counsel first of the permanent officials, I fear that I should had had all the enthusiasm (such as it is) knocked out of me.*[6]

Campbell-Bannerman remained in the War Office until 1875. Preoccupation with finance meant he was only obliquely involved with the last tranche of Cardwell reforms – the reorganisation of the line infantry. Cardwell created the county regiments with fixed depots in the places whose names they bore. One battalion served at home and one abroad – and abroad usually meant India – while a third territorial battalion was raised with the obligation to defend, when called upon to do so, the territories of the United Kingdom. The shape of the army remained very much as Cardwell had made it until the slaughter of the First World War. Then the politicians began to wonder if national morale could stand the concentrated anguish of a town which suffered the loss of so many of its sons on a single day.

The first Gladstone administration lost the general election of January 1874. The Grand Old Man himself – then only 65 – resigned the leadership of the Liberal Party a year later. In Opposition CB retained his interest in military matters. House of Commons debates which concern the armed forces of the Crown are rarely lively occasions. Votes of censure – particularly if they involve accusations of personal impropriety – invariably are. In May 1874 the two occasions coincided after Lord Sandhurst, a serving officer, was accused of drawing full pay and allowances while absent from his command.

As is the unhappy tradition of the House of Commons, although the question was theoretically non-partisan question of 'privilege', the speakers divided on party lines. One Tory alleged that, if corruption there had been it was at the direct behest of the defeated Liberal government. The logic of his accusation – that sums had been 'extorted' from Lord Sandhurst 'in order to reduce the estimates' – was less clear that the vehemence with which it was made. Campbell-Bannerman – his own honour in question – thought it necessary to reply. If the late government had acted corruptly, it could only have done so with the connivance of his Royal Highness the Commander-in-Chief. That was an indictment which he knew no Tory MP would be prepared to endorse. The careful construction of his argument surprised no-one. The irony with which he completed his speech was more unexpected. One of the more improbable accusations was that the government had made Sandhurst a peer on the understanding that, in the House of Lords, he would help to secure the passing of the Army (Commission) Purchase Bill. If that were so, said CB, ministers had made a most unfortunate miscalculation. Lord Sandhurst had spoken against the Bill. The accusation was withdrawn and the vote of censure collapsed in a gale of unanticipated laughter.

Gladstone, although theoretically in retirement, could not resist the impulse to thunder his opinions on great moral questions. And he saw moral implication in issues which other politicians regarded as raising only issues of competence. One was the Regimental Exchange Bill of 1875, a comparative minor adjustment to the method of making military appointments, which provoked an outburst which Disraeli, then Prime Minister, reported to the Queen. 'Mr Gladstone

W.E.Gladstone.

not only appeared but rushed into the debate. New Members trembled and fluttered like small birds when a hawk is in the air.' CB also saw the Bill as raising crucial ethical questions. It would, he claimed, *work evil in the army* by giving *a direct money value to the patronage of the Commander-in-Chief for an appointment in a home regiment.* He took the view that it was *not desirable that men should be induced to enter public service for gain but to do their duty to their country.*[7]

Campbell-Bannerman's House of Commons reputation – in so much as he possessed one – was for solid competence, invincible common sense and sympathy with the established order. He supported, in principle, Gladstone's position on the Eastern Question, though when his late leader put down a resolution urging the government to join Russia in driving the Turks 'bag and baggage ... from the province they have desolated and profaned', he sided with the Marquis of Hartington, Gladstone's successor, in arguing that sympathy for Greece should not be translated into military intervention on that country's behalf. He was critical of Disraeli's notion of having the Queen proclaimed Empress of India because of the quintessentially establishment conviction that *We cannot add to the lustre and dignity of the Crown of this realm, the most ancient and august in Europe, by tricking it out in a brand new title.*[8] He also feared that the Prince of Wales might, in consequence of his mother's new grandeur, come to be called the Prince Imperial – a shocking rejection of our island's history.

It is not unusual for politicians of a radical disposition to fall under the spell of the Royal Family. But there was one incident during CB's first experience of opposition which is less easily explained. In March 1878, with Cardwell in the Lords and therefore chief opposition spokesman on military affairs, Campbell-Bannerman wrote to Hartington with his advice on the reorganisation of the artillery. The Liberal Party, he argued, should oppose the introduction of breech-loaders. *Long and patient enquiry with overwhelming weight of authority have led to the retention of muzzle loaders ... Strength, safety, simplicity, economy, all in favour ... Rapidity of fire at least equal.*[9] The late 1870s were not CB's finest radical hours. For a moment the radical instinct either slept or was suppressed.

Nor was it a time at which even his friends anticipated that he would rise to the great heights of government. T P O'Connor wrote, with candid affection: 'Seated on the Front Opposition Bench, regularly but not too frequently, speaking only when the War Office Vote was under discussion and then speaking with hesitancy, without much emphasis and without the prestige of a great position and commanding oratory, he never attracted to the House a large audience, never raised a ripple of disturbance or enthusiasm on its surface.' [10]

It was therefore hardly surprising that in March 1877 Hugh Childers wrote to his wife, 'Two days ago Hartington asked me if I had any objection to take up army affairs, nobody but Campbell-Bannerman knowing anything about them on our bench'.[11] The suggestion that CB was regarded as an inad-

> Both the Army and Navy had rushed to adopt Armstrong breech-loading guns in the 1860s, but they had been found wanting in performance, and both services had reverted to muzzle-loading rifled guns. By the late 1870s, the problems of breech design had been solved, but it would not be until 1885 that the Army would commence the re-equipment of its field batteries with breech-loading guns. To be fair to CB, however, it would not be until the introduction of modern quick-firing artillery in the late 1890s that the practical rate of fire of breech-loading guns would greatly surpass that of muzzle-loaders.

equate spokesman was justified by subsequent events. When the Liberals returned to office, it was Childers, not CB, who became Secretary of State for War.

Chapter 2: An Excellent Administration

If Campbell-Bannerman's parliamentary career stagnated or – since immobility is failure in politics – went into decline, his personal life prospered. In 1872 his move from Queen's Gate to Eaton Square had made him next-door neighbour to Cardwell and confirmed his social standing. In 1878 the move to Grosvenor Place was financed by the inheritance which had followed his father's death. The Strathcathro estate went to his elder brother. But he received the house in Brunswick Street, £25,000 and the very considerable collection of family silver. Added to the bequest from Uncle Bannerman, the legacy made him a very rich man.

In 19th-century Britain the political pendulum swung with a predictable regularity. So it was assumed that, when the 1874 Parliament came to an end, the Liberals would sweep back to power. A year before the last due date for an election, Mr Gladstone re-emerged as the dominant force in the party by conducting the wholly unauthorised, in some ways idiosyncratic but in every particular brilliant, Midlothian Campaign during which he excoriated Benjamin Disraeli and denounced his foreign policy in a series of public meetings which attracted the biggest crowds ever recorded in a British political campaign. Some of them were held outside railway stations, enabling Gladstone to arrive on one train and address his host of admirers and supporters before leaving on the next. When he visited Dunfermline, CB was there on the platform with a gift of local linen for Mrs Gladstone.

The Liberals won the 1880 election with an overall majority – including the Irish Nationalists who supported the government in the hope of it introducing Home Rule – of 176. When the new government was formed, Campbell-Bannerman was offered, and accepted, the job from which the defeat of 1874 had removed him. He became Childers' Financial Secretary at the War Office and remained, in the estimation of the Secretary of State, 'an excellent administrator and economist'.[1] In those days 'economists' were not practitioners of the gloomy science but enthusiasts for reduced spending. Whether or not the implied reservation was intended, that was faint praise indeed when measured against the glittering talents of Joseph Chamberlain and Randolph Churchill, the two parliamentary contemporaries who were picked out as future prime ministers but who were to be beaten in the race for Downing Street by the plodding Campbell-Bannerman.

The two years of CB's second spell at the War Office were a time of mixed fortunes for the army. The attempt permanently to annex the Transvaal was abandoned after defeat by the Boers at Majuba Hill – like Isandhlwana in the Zulu Wars, not regarded as a reason to modify the claim of British military invincibility. The historic dispute between the Secretary of State and the Commander-in-Chief broke out again in 1881 when Childers chose, for appointment as Adjutant General, Sir Garnet Wolseley, an officer much admired by Campbell-Bannerman ever since they had served together in Cardwell's reforming ministry. Wolseley was delayed in taking up his appointment by the need to send him to Egypt to put down the Arabi Pasha revolt. His victory at Tel-el-Kebir won him a baronetcy, promotion to full general, a £30,000 gift of

THE SCHOOL OF MUSKETRY.

BOER (to F.-M. H. R. H. THE COMMANDER-IN-CHIEF). "I SAY, DOOK! YOU DON'T HAPPEN TO WANT A PRACTICAL
'MUSKETRY INSTRUCTOR,' DO YOU?"

thanks from Parliament and, perhaps most important to a professional soldier, immortality in a military catch-phrase: 'All Sir Garnet' came to mean that nothing was likely to go wrong. CB sent a note of congratulations from Marienbad. Wolseley replied that he hoped that 'we have now silenced the old fogies who, for some years past, have talked so much nonsense about young soldiers and the iniquity of those who favour army reform'. It was not the last battle for progress that they would fight together.

Despite the pleasure of even brief vindication, promotion to the Admiralty when it came in May 1882 must have been a relief as well as a pleasure. As Parliamentary as well as Financial Secretary he had an undoubted locus in the determination of policy. And his prestige was enhanced by the absence of Northbrook, the First Lord of the Admiralty, in the Upper House. His response to the congratulations which he received was modestly ambiguous. *It is, of course, a great piece of promotion and being my own master in the House will make it much more interesting. But it is a shocking grind to have to get up all the complicated technical details of a service of which I know nothing.*[2]

It is a shocking grind to have to get up all the complicated technical details of a service of which I know nothing.

CAMPBELL-BANNERMAN

He had to learn quickly. W T Stead, editor of the *Pall Mall Gazette*, was leading a campaign which claimed that the navy was under-strength and unprepared and demanded a major increase in naval expenditure. When John Morley, a previous *Pall Mall Gazette* editor, had been made Irish Secretary, Gladstone had asked him if he felt confident of his ability to deal with the murderous Fenians. Morley had replied that, after managing Stead for three years, no task daunted him. Stead was a pioneer of 'new journalism', a process by which journalists contributed to the stories about which they reported. The normal *modus operandi* was the promotion of a campaign which was said to be aimed at righting a wrong, exposing a scandal or revealing uncomfortable truths about public policy which the government preferred to conceal. Stead had already mounted one highly successful crusade. He had been an early critic of Disraeli's Eastern policy and helped to stimulate Gladstone into denouncing the Turks by sending him copies of articles on the subject from the *Northern Echo* which he then edited. His campaign for increased naval expenditure – backed up with the claim that the obsolete fleet could no longer adequately defend Britain – had less moral and factual justification.

Stead was supported in his demands by two men whose motives were certainly dubious and probably disreputable. Reginald Brett – one day to become Lord Esher, a favourite at the court of Queen Victoria – was secretary to Lord Hartington, the Secretary of State for War. Captain J A Fisher of HMS *Excellent* was a serving officer who was regarded by the Lords of the Admiralty as possessing the qualities which were essential to high command. They were right. 'Jackie' Fisher eventually became First Sea Lord. But in 1884 his behaviour, had it become public, would

John Arbuthnot Fisher (1841–1920) was the most influential naval reformer of the late 19th and early 20th century. At the Admiralty from 1892, he oversaw the development of the torpedo and submarines, the scrapping of obsolete ships, the improvement of training and dockyard organisation, and from 1905 the introduction of the 'all-big-gun' Dreadnought battleship which made all existing capital ships obsolete at a stroke. He retired as First Sea Lord in 1910, but returned to the post on the outbreak of war in 1914. He resigned in 1915 in opposition to the attack on Turkey at Gallipoli.

have warranted a court martial. Having supplied Stead with much highly dubious information he told him, 'You have got enough in your wallet to break half the officers in Her Majesty's Service if you split.'

The campaign began with an article in the *Pall Mall Gazette*, 'The Truth about the Navy by One who Knows the Facts'. Other newspapers took up the theme and produced their own variations on the basic allegation that shortage of funds had left our naval ports undefended and prevented the addition to the fleet of torpedo boats, one of Fisher's obsessions. The Tory opposition called for a public enquiry.

There is no way of knowing how Campbell-Bannerman felt, faced with a potential crisis at a time when the new First Lord of the Admiralty was in Upper Egypt and therefore unable to decide how to respond. He should have been elated. The opportunity to deputise ought to be the constant hope of deputies. Whether or not he welcomed the chance to take the crucial decisions, he grasped his good fortune by behaving with the maturity of a senior minister.

Hugh Childers, his old chief, had become Chancellor of the Exchequer. CB wrote to him in terms which, while making clear that there was no cause for either political or strategic panic, some action was necessary both to allay public disquiet and to make essential improvements in the navy's capabilities.

Although I do not believe that the hysterical excitement of the Pall Mall Gazette *extends far beyond London, there is sufficient interest and anxiety felt in the country to prevent the question being shelved or postponed ... the opposition will support a motion insisting on the Navy being strengthened and whatever its motives may be (as to which I have no idea) many of our people will join them.*[3]

Campbell-Bannerman's solution was an increase on naval expenditure of *half a million to a million*. In conformity with good ministerial practice he offered, as a protection to the Chancellor, a full review of naval expenditure during the previous 20 years. But he added, as both a cautionary note and an incentive to greater expenditure, that Britain's capacity for making armour plate and torpedoes was far inferior to that of France. The Cabinet was so impressed by his arguments that it authorised a supplementary naval estimate of £3 million. The result was two new battleships and 13 new cruisers.

Within days of the Cabinet's decision to increase the Naval Estimates, the Parliamentary Secretary to the Admiralty gained the just reward for a task completed with the calm efficiency that always impresses politicians. Campbell-Bannerman was appointed Chief Secretary for Ireland. Northbrook wrote from Cairo to express his despair at losing so loyal a lieutenant. Wolseley, in the Nubian desert, described CB's new job as 'more difficult than taking a small army to Khartoum' and added, gratuitously CB must have thought, that 'to be a Scotchman [is] to the Irish Nationalists worse even than being English'. Rosebery was equally pessimistic but added that the new Chief Secretary should take joy in one aspect of his promotion. 'You have now an opportunity of displaying those great talents which I have long known you to possess.' CB was not a man to be disheartened by the difficulty of the task ahead. But in one particular he was deeply disappointed. He was not to sit in the Cabinet.

'You have now an opportunity of displaying those great talents which I have long known you to possess.'

ROSEBERY TO CAMPBELL-BANNERMAN

He inherited a difficult legacy. Three years earlier the government had been in direct and bitter conflict with an increasingly militant Home Rule movement. In October 1881 Gladstone had told a banquet in his honour in Leeds that

'the resources of civilisation are not yet exhausted' – meaning that Fenian terror would be combated with the rifle and the sword. In reply, Charles Stewart Parnell had announced that any Irishman who laid down his arms 'placed himself in the power of the perfidious, cruel and relentless British enemy'. Parnell was arrested, charged and imprisoned under the Coercion Acts. But in May 1882 he had been released from Kilmainham Gaol after a secret pact – negotiated through Captain O'Shea, the husband of Parnell's mistress – in which the government agreed to abandon coercion and the Parnellites condemned violence. As was always the case when an Irish Nationalist spoke up for moderation, more extreme elements thought it necessary to demonstrate that reason did not prevail throughout the country. Four days after Parnell was released from gaol, Lord Cowper, the Lord Lieutenant, and Lord Frederic Cavendish, the Chief Secretary, were murdered in Phoenix Park. Charles Dilke was invited to become Chief Secretary and declined because he regarded the offer, without a seat in the Cabinet, as an insult. George Trevelyan was appointed in his place. He served for two turbulent years during which the renewed violence was so constant and widespread that a new Coercion Act was the only way of bringing peace to the province. It failed. And the Opposition blamed the government for its failure.

Trevelyan's tenure ended in something approaching a nervous breakdown. Earl Spencer, the Viceroy of Ireland and, as the Queen's representative senior to the Chief Secretary, wrote to the Prime Minister with 'the conclusion that in the public interest it is most desirable that Trevelyan should be relieved of his post ... He has lost his nerve with Irish MPs.' Spencer – looking for a safe pair of hands – concluded that 'either S Lefevre or Campbell-Bannerman could fill the post with success'.[4]

Shaw Lefevre was approached but expressed reservations about the coercion policy. Despite doubts about his willingness to *exchange his present congenial post at the Admiralty for the horribly thankless office of Chief Secretary*, Campbell-Bannerman was summoned to Edinburgh where Spencer (the Viceroy) rather than Gladstone (the Prime Minister) offered him the job. CB declined. Spencer's letter to Downing Street explained that CB 'professed entire ignorance of Irish affairs and said that he had never faced any formidable Parliamentary foes and had no confidence that he would succeed'. The number of formidable opponents was about to increase. Household suffrage had been extended from the cities to the counties by the 1884 Reform Bill. From then on, Ireland sent to Westminster Members of Parliament who represented agrarian discontent and the related demand for Home Rule. Spencer suggested that CB spent a night in reflection on 'the merits of coming to a different conclusion', but he telegraphed Mr Gladstone to express 'the fear that he will not change his mind'.

CB had his mind changed for him. Charlotte, told that he was finding the definite letter of refusal difficult to write, suggested that he 'could not write it because it is a false letter'. His conscience told him that it was his duty to accept. The acceptance arrived almost too late. Sir Henry James, the third choice, had already been told to stand by for a call to Downing Street. But after some embarrassed conversation with the Viceroy – who had decided that he preferred James after all – Gladstone decided that the offer to CB must stand. However, he could not have felt much enthusiasm for the appointment or faith in his eventual choice. James would have been given a seat in the Cabinet. When consideration was given to doing the same for Campbell-Bannerman, Lord Charles Grosvenor, the government Chief Whip, argued, 'It is much better that he should not be in so that if he gets into a mess with the Irish in the House of Commons, it is much easier to throw him over.'[5]

The appointment was greeted with even less enthusiasm in Ireland. Tim Healey was particularly aggressive. 'Mr Campbell-Bannerman is one of those who have the insufferable egoism ... To go over and pretend to rule five millions of people, not one of whom they saw before, on whose shores they have never landed and of whose history and feelings they are entirely ignorant.'[6] But T P O'Connor began to feel a grudging admiration. 'It might have been self confidence. It was probably indifference. But there was no human being who seemed so absolutely impervious to attack ... He laughed at vituperation. He was jaunty under a cyclone of attacks'.[7]

'He [CB] laughed at vituperation. He was jaunty under a cyclone of attacks.'

T P O'CONNOR

CB's exclusion from the Cabinet Office obliged him to defend policies which he had no part in making – sometimes policies with which he did not agree. His innate radicalism was more often expressed in private than in public. He told Spencer that he was opposed to a law which resulted *in a man being tried merely for being a Fenian*. But he felt sufficiently confident to announce in Parliament, *With regard to jury packing ... I think the House generally would wish that extraordinary care should be taken against the wholesale setting aside of Catholics*. He sent a memorandum to the Cabinet arguing that *stopping meetings does, in the vast majority of cases, far more harm than good*.[8] There followed desultory work on a new Coercion Bill – with Mr Gladstone objecting to its title but not its content – and a Land Purchase Bill by which public money would be used to buy out landlords and divide their property amongst the peasantry. A bill to extend elementary

education to Ireland – introduced by CB with the proud claim that he had been in favour of compulsory universal education since 1869 – had more success. But every measure promised for Ireland was really no more than a reflection of the issue which had convulsed the country for a century and was to convulse it for another hundred years. The real question was Home Rule.

The death of General Gordon at Khartoum – in the mind of the public deserted by Mr Gladstone – meant that the administration was doomed. But, as was so often the case in the 19th century, defeat was, at least technically, the result of shifting alliances within Parliament. Joseph Chamberlain, with the success of the Liberal Caucus on the Birmingham Town Council still fresh in his memory, proposed the election of a Central Board to run Irish education, the poor law and public works. It was to be elected, not by popular franchise, but by County Boards which should fulfil the other functions of local government. CB had the strongest doubts about the scheme's practicability – particularly the conflict which he felt bound to arise between the chairman of the board and Westminster ministers. Most of the Cabinet felt the same. Denied even such a limited measure of devolution, Parnell withdrew his support from the Liberal government. On 8 June 1885, budget resolutions were defeated, Gladstone resigned and Lord Salisbury formed a Tory administration.

Campbell-Bannerman spent the autumn in Marienbad. In the general election of November he was returned to Parliament unopposed. His address to the people of the Stirling Burghs promised support for *a large extension of local self-government in Ireland* but opposed *separation under one name or another*. During the debates which followed in the new parliament, CB insisted that he was not an opponent of Home Rule which, he insisted, was quite different from the outright independence which some Irish nationalists demanded. Gladstone, who knew exactly what he wanted for Ireland, hoped that the constitutional change would be proposed by the new Conservative government, allowing him to offer the Tories the unequivocal support which he would not promise in advance. On 14 December 1885, the Cabinet considered a proposal for the Earl of Carnarvon (Spencer's successor as Viceroy) that there should be an immediate movement towards Home Rule – and rejected it. If Ireland's problems were to be solved by a new constitutional settlement, only the Liberals would provide it.

Two days after the Tory Cabinet had rejected Home Rule, Spencer wrote to Campbell-Bannerman suggesting an urgent meeting. 'Mr Gladstone may write to me or see me and I am in real anxiety… '. Before it was held, CB told the *Daily News* of his regret that it was too late for *the matter to be raised out of the area of party strife*, and Queen Victoria's Private Secretary noted in his diary that he had always supported 'Campbell-Bannerman's suggestion that there should be a union of parties to deal with the Irish question … And when I told HM, she agreed'.

CB's statement to the *Daily News* was never of a sufficiently original nature to capture the headlines. But had it been twice as sensational, it would have been overshadowed by an interview which Herbert Gladstone, W E's son, gave to the National Press Agency on the same day, after being told by Wemyss Reid, the Liberal editor of the *Leeds Mercury*, that the parties in the country must be given guidance about Ireland's future. The *Pall Mall Gazette*, more authoritative and less sensational than usual, wrote 'Mr Gladstone has definitely adopted the policy of Home Rule for Ireland and there are well founded hopes that he will win over the moderate section of the party to his views'. It now seems that Gladstone had decided, during the Midlothian Campaign, that the only way forward was an Irish parliament which took responsibility for domestic affairs in a province which remained part of the Union. But he had kept his conversion to himself. His son's announcement outraged the Liberal establishment – including many members of the recently defeated Cabinet who supported the idea but resented their support being taken for granted. Fortunately for Gladstone, the government was also deeply split between coercion and conciliation. After the life of barely a year, it was defeated, certainly by surprise and almost by mistake, during the debate on the Queen's Speech on 21 January 1886.

The defeat was – formally at least – on an amendment moved by Jesse Collings, a Birmingham MP who is otherwise only notable for laying the foundation stone of that great city's Council House. It regretted the absence of 'any measure benefiting the rural labourer' – a parliamentary way of advocating the generalised ownership of 'two acres and a cow', the policy advocated by his hero, Joe Chamberlain, in his 'alternative programme'. But any government defeat on the Queen's Speech is lethal. The Liberals were back in office.

Chapter 3: 'A Good Honest Scotchman at the War Office'

At last CB was awarded a place in the Cabinet. It came very largely as a result of royal patronage. Gladstone wanted Childers back at the War Office. But during the previous Liberal administration, he had been at constant logger-heads with the Commander-in-Chief, His Royal Highness the Duke of Cambridge who, being the Queen's cousin, was able to organise majestic opposition to his re-appointment. The message from Downing Street to Windsor was grudgingly explicit. The Prime Minister agreed 'at great sacrifice to give up Mr Childers and select the gentleman named by Your Majesty, Mr Campbell-Bannerman. The Commander-in-Chief retained happy memories of CB's work as Financial Secretary. He had convinced the Queen that the down-to-earth 'administrator' would leave the army (and the position of Commander-in-Chief) undisturbed. So Victoria recorded her pleasure, as well as her victory over the detested Mr Gladstone, in her diary. We have, she wrote, 'a good honest Scotchman at the War Office'.

Two pieces of Liberal folklore followed. The first was that CB, seated in close proximity to the Prime Minister at his first Cabinet meeting, was too overawed to speak. The second is that Gladstone put him at his ease by speaking in the patois of a Scottish peasant. In introducing Cabinet colleagues he

proclaimed, 'You'll get on all right with them. You will be canny and you will be couthy'. Both stories are inherently improbable.

CB had spent much of Christmas writing to colleagues about what the Liberal Party's Irish policy should be. He was not sure that Home Rule *would be accepted as satisfactory and final* and wondered if men of goodwill could rely *on the moderates standing firm.* But, referring to his doubts about the practicability of the 'Central Board' solution, he conceded, *whatever difficulties and dangers may attend a separate parliament, it does not create the conditions of antagonism in administration which I dreaded in the scheme of last summer.* Anticipating the opposition of the *Times*, most Liberals and many radicals, he concluded that *the scheme of separate parliament is impractical for the moment.* Mr Gladstone took a more heroic view. And Mr Gladstone was wrong. The government was doomed from the start. The 'aristocratic element' within the Liberal Party declined to accept office. Joe Chamberlain joined but resigned. The Home Rule Bill introduced on 8 April was defeated by 341 votes to 311.

It had been assumed that Campbell-Bannerman, who spoke on the second day of the debate, would announce concessions aimed at persuading the least die-hard dissidents to rally to the government's cause. But all he did was to give already anticipated assurances about the rights of Irish interests in the Westminster parliament. The speech was on the whole badly received inside and outside the House. Perhaps he was lucky that the government was doomed. It fell after barely a year in office. His failure in one of the great debates of the century was forgotten in opposition.

Ireland festered on with coercion bill following coercion bill and land act following land act. Gladstone, accompanied by CB, had explorative talks with Parnell, the leader of the

A WAITING GAME.

H-RT-NGT-N. "HULLO, RANDOLPH! WHAT'S YOUR LITTLE GAME *NOW?*"
R-ND-LPH (*Aside—sotto voce*). "ALL RIGHT! WANT HIM TO SHOW HIS HAND!"

Irish Party, in early 1890, rightly judging that no-one else could promote a peaceful transition to Home Rule. Then, in November, Parnell was suddenly removed from the political equation. Captain William O'Shea cited him as co-respondent in his divorce suit and the 'compact of the hearts' – the romantic description of the Irish Party which typified their impractical view of politics – was dissolved in Committee Room 14 of the House of Commons. Parnell had, for a while, hoped to hang on. Perhaps, had the Liberal Party Organisation not been holding its annual meeting in Sheffield – a hot-bed of Nonconformist piety – he might have survived. As it was, the puritans confounded the best hope of Irish peace. CB, in his letters to colleagues, represented the prejudices of the time in what now sounds like a satire on sanctimonious political pronouncements. He was, once more, censorious about the Irish leader's conduct. Mr Parnell was guilty of *a breach of the moral law (and) the exhibition of a shiftiness of character and want of straightforwardness*. For once, his judgement was categorically wrong. Unless Parnell resigned *a very serious blow would be struck at Home Rule policy*.[1]

In opposition CB continued his military connections, serving on the Hartington Committee which considered the reorganisation of the armed forces. Its first report recommended a unified defence ministry, an idea which, killed by CB among others, was not accepted by either serving officers or politicians until 1963. It was another example of Campbell-Bannerman's limitations. His strength was common sense, not inspiration. The Committee's proposal to abolish the post of Commander-in-Chief was shelved – its implementation depended on the appointment of a Secretary of State who recognised what common sense demanded.

Gladstone took office for the fourth and last time in August 1892, after Queen Victoria had eventually 'made up her mind to send for that dreadful old man'. Once again the Duke of Cambridge expressed the hope that CB would be appointed Secretary of State – repeating the strange procedure by which the Commander-in-Chief chose the minister rather than vice versa. Wolseley – Commander-in-Chief in Ireland – began at once to canvass for changes in the army, particularly promotion on merit rather than by seniority. The Duke resisted. But he was not the only obstacle to change. The Queen refused point-blank to allow 'her' foot guards to serve abroad and demanded the creation of a second battalion of Cameron Highlanders – a regiment which recruited most of its men in the East End of London. CB resisted demands by Lord Roberts to be made Commanding Officer at Aldershot but then had to deflect suggestions from the Queen that the Duke of Connaught be appointed in preparation for one royal duke to succeed another as Commander-in-Chief of the Army. The duke she had in mind was her son.

CB remained faithful to the recommendations of the Hartington Committee of which he had been a member – but only in a modified form. The post of Commander-in-Chief should, in his opinion, be retained in a much modified (that is to say less influential) form. But he had no doubt that it should no longer be occupied by the Duke of Cambridge who was then 76. Cambridge was ready to go – but not at the time determined by the Secretary of State. The Queen, who accepted the inevitability of her cousin's retirement, would have positively welcomed it had her son been chosen to succeed him. Her fear was not that the Duke of Connaught might have to wait but that, before she could arrange his appointment, the office would be abolished in favour of one of the many proposals for reform – an Army Board, based on the Board of Admiralty and a First Army Lord with powers parallel to those of the First Sea Lord. CB calmed her fears by assuring Her Majesty that her royal hope would one day be realised. The note of the meeting records a demonstration of impeccable tact.

'Saw Mr C Bannerman ... Who thought the C in C's retiring a good idea as would stifle spirit of discontent in H of C. D of C now succeeding to C in C practically impossible. But after some other general has held it for a term, not exceeding 5 years, HRH would then be received with acclamation.'

Next day the Queen saw the Duke of Cambridge who said, in all sincerity, it was his concern that the post should be kept so as to insulate the army from political interference and that it should be held by an officer whose only allegiance was to the person of the sovereign. Victoria had become the advocate of CB's reform and had achieved his purpose. A private secretary was sent to Aldershot to break the bad news to General the Duke of Connaught.

The change in Commander-in-Chief was not the biggest Whitehall upheaval of the time. William Ewart Gladstone – after four terms as Prime Minister – had resigned his office, unwilling to accept increases in the Naval Estimates which his Cabinet demanded. Supported by Sir William Harcourt, the Chancellor of the Exchequer, Gladstone had also demanded reductions in the Army Estimates. CB argued that it was impossible to go below the previous year's figure but agreed to a cut of £3 million. Harcourt continued to press for more reductions. Everyone else wanted spending to increase. Gladstone actually intervened during a House of Commons debate to announce his refusal to spend more on the Volunteers. CB, speaking later, accepted that more money needed to be spent on the part-time recruits. But it was not the disagreement between the Secretary of State for War and the Prime Minister which ended the career of the Grand Old Man. That was not CB's way. He would, if necessary, have compromised. But the Admiralty stood firm. Gladstone resigned and new Estimates were prepared. Gladstone was succeeded by Lord Rosebery – a mercurial, some would say manic, one-time devotee of the Grand Old Man. His strength was not being Harcourt, a clearly superior intellect whose brilliance was only matched by his unpopularity with his colleagues. Harcourt had no doubt that he should have been chosen to lead the party and only agreed to join the government – which would have fallen had he not agreed to do so – after Rosebery agreed to make him both Chancellor of the Exchequer and Leader of the House of Commons, with power to call Cabinet meetings at his own discretion. The difference in the two men's character is demonstrated by their rival attitude to the political vocation. Harcourt wrote, 'When I am ill, I am in bed. When I am not, I am in the House of Commons'. Rosebery said, 'There are two supreme pleasures of life. One is ideal, the other is real. The ideal is when a man receives the Seals of Office from his Sovereign. The real is when he hands them back.' It was clear that the Rosebery Administration would not last for long. It came to an end on the day that the Duke's retirement was announced.

After weeks of delicate negotiations, the situation remained unresolved. CB told the Prime Minister, *The Duke is, I believe, being urged by his own family … not on any account to give way in face of vulgar attacks … He declares a strong repugnance to resignation … even if requested by H M … It would be showing the white feather.*[2] That notwithstanding, Campbell-Bannerman thought that he would initiate his own resignation to *save his dignity*. CB was wrong. His next note admitted his error. *My old Duke wrote* [the Queen] *a letter which did not quite tally with what he told me.* Victoria, by now wholly on the side of the 'kind and sensible Mr C Bannerman', acted (wildly out of character) as the government's agent. But 'George C ... would not see the reason for resigning.' Then the volatile C in C changed his mind again. 'CB saw the Duke again and found him quite tired out ... He seemed quite agreeable' to the suggestion that his annual visit to Homburg would be an ideal opportunity for a resignation announcement. Cambridge still havered. So, in May 1895, the Queen sent him what amounted to a notice to quit. 'I have come to the conclusion on the advice of my officers ... that for your own sake as well as in the public interest, it is inexpedient that you should not much longer retain that position from which I think you should be relieved at the end of your autumn duties.'[3]

Vacillation was replaced by procrastination. The Duke argued about the date of his resignation, the statement which was to accompany it and the pension to which he was due, in addition to his salary as Colonel of the Grenadier Guards (£2,000 a year) and his allowance from the Privy Purse (£12,000 a year) and a rent- and rate-free Grace and Favour house. The Queen shared the Cabinet's view that 'a pension would be preposterous' but knowing that her cousin hoped for a valedictory title, told the Prime Minister, 'The Office and Title of Grand Master of the Order of the Bath is in abeyance, as I did not wish anyone to hold it after my husband. Would that please the Duke?'

On 20 June 1895 CB told the House of Commons that the Duke had decided to lay down his heavy burden. The new Commander-in-Chief would have more limited duties and a fixed tenure in the post. His essential role would be chief military adviser to the Secretary of State. He would be supported by an Adjutant General, a Quartermaster General, the Director of Artillery and Inspector General of Fortification, all of whom would report directly to the Secretary of State. The War Office had not been reorganised, but

the fundamental change had been made. The Secretary of State was in indisputable control. CB's letter to the Duke, expressing his gratitude for the *distinguished honour ... of serving the Queen as a colleague of YRH* contained a strange sentence. After referring to his statement in the House of Commons, CB observed, *the incident which occurred later in the evening will probably lead to the severance of my connection with the War Office.*[4]

The 'incident' was a snap defeat of the government on a motion to reduce Campbell-Bannerman's salary. The 'scandal' to which it referred was, as is usually the case with such motions, very largely invented. And the trap was set and sprung – with equally typical cynicism – not because of the opposition's real concern but because the government was in such a debilitated state that it needed only a touch to make it fall. The tottering government was pushed over on the day of CB's statement about the retirement of the Commander-in-Chief – clearly the most important business on the Order Paper. But it was not the treatment of the Old Duke which presented the Tories with the opportunity for an ambush. It was the claim – justified or bogus – that the army was short of cordite.

St John Broderick, a Tory MP who specialised in military affairs, had heard a rumour that, because of a lack of cordite, in a national emergency ammunition might be insufficient for the army's needs. He wrote to CB with a request for information which suggested that his only concern was the national interest. CB consulted General Buller who assured him that 'there is no shortage and no case to be met'. Broderick consulted Arthur Balfour and Lord Salisbury – the Tories'

leaders in the Commons and Lords. Conscious of CB's popularity – and anxious not to mount a failed coup – they agreed to the subject being raised on the floor of the House if Joseph Chamberlain could be persuaded to throw the weight of the Liberal Unionists behind the vote of censure. Chamberlain refused.

Then CB answered War Office questions in the House of Commons. One concerned two Highlanders who had died of sunstroke on a route march. Members suggested that their deaths were the result of soldiers being required to wear 'the absurd forage cap'. Campbell-Bannerman, in what was clearly as a moment of madness, chose to respond with what can only be described as a joke – a weak joke, but a joke nevertheless. *We have taken away from the British soldier my native Glengary. Perhaps it was owing to that this melancholy event occurred*. CB then made his statement on the retirement of the old Duke. But the real business of the day was going on outside the chamber. Broderick convinced Chamberlain that no other minister could get away with such insensitivity and that Campbell-Bannerman should not be allowed to escape.

Cordite began to replace black powder in ammunition from 1889, as it was more powerful and did not produce clouds of smoke. The name derived from the 'cords' or rods the compound of nitroglycerine, guncotton and petroleum jelly was extruded in. Thinner cords burnt faster and were used for small-arms ammunition, while larger-diameter ones burnt more slowly and were used in artillery rounds. The elimination of smoke allowed higher practical rates of fire, as the target would not be obscured after the first few rounds, thus facilitating the development of both quick-firing artillery and machine guns.

So the Tories moved the motion which proposed a reduction

of £100 in the salary of the Secretary of State for War. The Financial Secretary to the War Office assured the House that there was no shortage of cordite. CB spoke twice – once confirming that he could mobilise three army corps *and had sufficient ammunition for all of them* and once again unwisely suggesting that concern was greatest among Members of Parliament with cordite factories in their constituencies. The speech was not a great success, for CB was not at his best when he was required to extemporise and it seemed that he had not anticipated so fierce an attack. The second intervention – made after both Balfour, the Leader of the Opposition, and Joe Chamberlain had spoken – was the most counterproductive. Instead of relying on lofty denials he grubbed about among details of cordite orders and suppliers. In a half-empty House the government was defeated by seven votes – 132 to 125.

Campbell-Bannerman moved the adjournment of the House and immediately left the chamber muttering, *You must find another Secretary of State*. The government could have reversed the vote – even though the loss of CB was probably unavoidable. But morale was low. Majorities had been small during the committee stage of the bill which aimed at disestablishing the Welsh Church. And Rosebery, the Prime Minister, was of a melancholic disposition which encouraged him to agree with Harcourt's telegram. 'It is a chance blow, but a fatal one'. The only argument between ministers concerned whether to resign and let the Tories form a government or dissolve Parliament and fight a general election. A majority eventually coalesced around resignation. Rosebery, in tending his resignation to the Queen, offered the opinion that the Tories had behaved badly and the Queen told him 'That the government should be defeated by an attack on the most popular of its Members is too extraordinary.' However, constitutional duty had to be done. On the evening of Rosebery's resignation, she sent for Salisbury who advised an immediate dissolution.

There followed one of the strangest episodes in British constitutional history. The Cabinet which had agreed to – indeed insisted upon – the Duke of Cambridge's resignation, had decided that General Sir Redvers Buller should succeed him as Commander-in-Chief but had not announced its decision to pass over Field Marshal Lord Roberts and Sir Garnet Wolseley. The Tories wanted Wolseley and Salisbury feared that, in the hiatus between Rosebery's resignation and the appointment of a new Cabinet, CB would use the authority which he still possessed to make Buller's appointment official. He therefore sent his private secretary to demand that the Secretary of State for War should hand his Seals of Office directly to Broderick rather than return them to the Queen. Of course, CB refused. But his sense of propriety also prevented him from using his residual authority to appoint Buller. Wolseley got the job.

Chapter 4: 'A Warming Pan Has its Uses'

The general election of 1895 was disastrous for the Liberals. Lord Salisbury's majority was 150 seats – the result of the number of Liberal members falling from 274 to 177. Sir William Harcourt and John Morley were both defeated, though Campbell-Bannerman increased his vote. Mr Gladstone, who had much disapproved of Rosebery's decision to capitulate rather than fight, told Margot Asquith, 'Your man is the man of the future'. Her husband, Home Secretary in the Rosebery government, had won golden opinions. It was generally assumed that it would not be long before a new party leader was elected and that the unanimous choice of successor would be Herbert Henry Asquith.

During the years of opposition, CB spoke mostly on military matters but increasingly about the imperial obligation which it was the army's duty to discharge. He was increasingly critical of what was called a 'forward' foreign policy – the belief that Britain should play a positive, and if necessary military, part in regulating the world. He spoke of Britain's influence in the world being dependent on maintaining *an Empire of peace and commerce and good relations* and urged the government to forswear *the military spirit which would destroy the character of our nation and Empire*.[1] Sometimes he crossed the line which divided the out-and-out radicals from the rest of the party. He even argued that non-commissioned officers should be commissioned more regularly, if necessary at the expense of the usual recruits from the sixth forms of public schools. Campbell-Bannerman has the distinction of being one of the few politicians of modern times to move to the left as a result of close association with the armed forces.

Although Asquith was what, these days, would be called the 'front-runner' in the as yet undeclared race to succeed Rosebery, Campbell-Bannerman was regarded as at least a contender for the Liberal crown. Even before Mr Gladstone resigned, the *Spectator* had reported that 'in the inner circle of Gladstonians' CB was said to be 'the only person capable of stilling the fierce conflicts of sects and interests [which was] certain to succeed the political demise of the present regime'. Within a month of the Prime Minister's resignation, Rosebery was in Downing Street and CB's claims to the succession had been submerged beneath talk of the irresistible attractions of John Morley and William Harcourt, the party's two 'intellectuals'. It seemed unlikely that, in their hour of need, the Liberals would turn to a plain man. And if CB had spent much time hoping that he would one day lead the nation, he clearly accepted that his moment had passed.

In the dying days of the Rosebery government, Campbell-Bannerman, with his reputation high both in the party and country, decided that he wanted to abandon at least taking part in the hurly-burly of parliamentary conflict and, instead, preside over it. He hoped to become Speaker of the House of Commons – a post which would have ended his career in active politics and a distinction to which few men who had held high ministerial office even aspire. There had been talk of him 'taking the chair' when the formidable Speaker Brand had retired in 1883, but the job had gone to Arthur Peel, son of Sir Robert. When the vacancy recurred 12 years later, CB – perhaps anticipating long years of opposition – made it clear that he was available.

The *Times* had supported his candidature but ended its endorsement with an expression of doubt that the job had much attraction 'for one who may be, at no distant day, the leader of his party'. But CB – perhaps disheartened by Rosebery's success – had pressed his claim with a letter to the Prime Minister which, while properly not *touching on the question of fitness* expressed a *strong personal desire to turn into this channel*. Rosebery's answer was flattering but disappointing. 'No minister, and of all ministers least of all you, can be spared to fill the Speakership'. CB honourably absented himself from the Cabinet which considered who it should support. It agreed that no minister should be nominated. After much canvassing of other candidates – willing and reluctant – the lot had fallen on William Gully who, among his other qualifications, was the grandson of the bare-knuckle prizefighting champion of England.

On 1 January 1896, an armed party of almost 700 men – under the leadership of Doctor Leander Star Jameson – left Mafeking and crossed the border into the Transvaal Republic. They believed that they would act as a catalyst which would induce the English settlers to rise up against their Boer oppressors. The English did not rise up and the Boers – a warlike if not martial people – disposed of the invasion within 48 hours. Cecil Rhodes, the Prime Minister of Cape Colony – who had certainly known about the raid in advance and probably helped in its organisation – resigned. Joe Chamberlain, the Colonial Secretary in Lord Salisbury's government, was suspected of being almost as complicit. Outrage in London turned to something embarrassingly close to sympathy when the Kaiser congratulated Paul

Le Petit Journal

Le Petit Journal
CHAQUE JOUR 5 CENTIMES

Le Supplément illustré
CHAQUE SEMAINE 5 CENTIMES

SUPPLÉMENT ILLUSTRÉ
Huit pages : CINQ centimes

ABONNEMENTS

SEINE ET SEINE-ET-OISE ... 2 fr. 3 fr. 50
DÉPARTEMENTS ... 2 fr. 4 fr.
ÉTRANGER ... 2 50 5 fr.

Septième année

DIMANCHE 19 JANVIER 1896

Numéro 270

AU TRANSVAAL
Le docteur Jameson prisonnier des Boers

Kruger, the President of the Transvaal, on his victory over the British.

It took the government and Parliament over a year to set up an enquiry into the origin of the raid. Salisbury had originally thought a Royal Commission appropriate but was persuaded – by Harcourt among others – that a Select Committee of the House of Commons would be more suitable. Since it was thought wrong for the committee to sit until Jameson's trial (held in London) was over, and because of the inability to hold meetings when Parliament was not in session, the proceedings did not begin until February 1897. Its members included Harcourt and Campbell-Bannerman and, rather more surprising, Joseph Chamberlain. The Liberal Party's position was complicated, though not quite compromised, by Lord Rosebery describing the raid as 'an Elizabethan adventure'.

The first witness was Cecil Rhodes himself who, such was the gentlemanly nature of the proceedings, was allowed to give evasive answers to most of the questions and failed completely to answer the rest. Chamberlain gave evidence to the committee of which he was a member and, perhaps not unsurprisingly, was acquitted of involvement in the raid. His exoneration was all the more extraordinary in the light of the discovery that Miss Flora Shaw of the *Times* had followed an interview with Colonial Office officers by telegraphing Rhodes with the news that she 'had special reason to believe' that the Colonial Secretary 'wishes you must do it immediately'. When she denied that her message implicated Chamberlain, CB offered a chivalrous justification for her unconvincing testimony. *One forgives the lady who sent* [the telegram] *in consideration of her zeal and excited temperament ... She probably did not realise the very powerful meaning which such an expression would have when it reached South Africa.* His reputation for common sense was restored with a comment about the whole governance of the Cape. *The government must have learned how dangerous it was to entrust the administration of a great territory to a trading company – or rather not to a trading company but to a speculative financial company.*[2] But he remained a reasonable radical. He complained that Labouchere – the 'progressive' who added to a bill outlawing child prostitution a clause making all homosexual acts a criminal offence – did *more to render the Committee ineffective than any other man. He was constantly running about declaring that he had got wonderful evidence which, when it was examined, always came to nothing.*[3]

The government must have learned how dangerous it was to entrust the administration of a great territory to a trading company – or rather not to a trading company but to a speculative financial company.

CAMPBELL-BANNERMAN

Despite the evidence of his frustration, it could not be said that he played a significant part in the attempt to reveal the truth about the raids. A great deal of evidence (condemning Rhodes and Chamberlain) was provided by a box of telegram duplicates, which one member of the raiding party had allowed to fall into the hands of the Boers. But when the British South Africa Company refused to release copies of their telegrams to Jameson, the Committee largely accepted the rebuff. The only reasonable conclusion was that most of its members, CB included, did not want to discover – indeed did not want to believe – that a Secretary of State and Privy Councillor had been part of a conspiracy to subvert a sovereign nation.

W E Gladstone died in May 1898. It had been five years since he led the Liberal Party and the country yet it was taken for granted that his death would cause a seismic shift in the disposition of political forces. Rosebery – who had once been such an admirer of Gladstone that he announced his unavailability for office lest his obvious attachment was interpreted as attempts to ingratiation – had become entirely disenchanted with the GOM's policies. He was totally opposed to Irish Home Rule and Gladstone's position on the Eastern Question and was fast moving towards support for 'imperial preference' which would impose duties on 'foreign' as distinct from 'empire' imports. Finding himself 'in apparent difference with a mass of the Liberal Party' he resigned the leadership. In the belief that a long period of opposition lay ahead, an interim solution was put in place. Sir William Harcourt would lead the Commons while Lord Kimberly led in the Lords. The device was short-lived. John Morley announced that he no longer wished to serve 'in the formal councils of the heads of the Liberal Party' and Harcourt, although effectively the leader of the whole opposition, was obviously not ready for the long haul which preceded power. He replied to Morley's resignation letter with what was essentially an abdication statement. 'My resolution is fixed to undertake no responsibility and occupy no position, the requirement of which it is made impossible for me to fulfil ... I am not, and shall not consent to be, a candidate in any contested position.' In fact, he had learned that the party's dissatisfaction with his interim leadership had grown to the point at which some of his parliamentary colleagues were hoping for the return of Lord Rosebery. He had decided to step down before he was forced out.

The agony of realignment and replacement had barely begun when political attention shifted from the internal workings of the opposition to the foreign policy of the government. On 2 September 1898, General Kitchener – who had advanced up the Nile, building a railway as he went – met the Dervish army at Khartoum. Thanks in part to the use of the machine gun, a recent military innovation, 10,000 tribesmen were slaughtered while only 300 British

... ... Fashoda.
... ... says France's
... Red Riding Hood. 'All the
... to eat your biscuit,' replies the
... tated and perfidious Albion. The
... over Fashoda was the nearest Great
... came to war between 1878 and 1911.
... British kept Fashoda—without allies
... actically without effort.

troops were killed or wounded. Gordon was avenged. But the celebration was interrupted by the discovery that a contingent of Senegalese troops, under the command of Captain Marchand, had planted the French tricolour at Fashoda on the White Nile.

In the dying days of the Rosebery government, Edward Grey, not yet the doyen of the Foreign Office which he became, had warned France that an intrusion into that part of Africa which was a British sphere of influence 'would be an unfriendly act and would be so viewed in England'. Salisbury endorsed that view and was supported by Rosebery. For a month, France and Britain were on the brink of war. CB – having argued that neither the French people nor the French government was to blame for what he agreed was an inflammatory act – declared that *the Fashoda Incident would never have occurred if Lord Rosebery had been our Foreign Secretary*.[4] The Liberal Imperialists were in head-on collision with the section of the party which, in the words of the National Federation Chairman 'would never drop themselves in the filthy mire of a spirited foreign policy'. It was a brief, if melodramatic, interlude in the Liberal Party's search for a new leader.

There were only two possible candidates in the minds of those who sought a new Liberal leader. Herbert Henry Asquith was the choice of those who wanted a new beginning. Although he had served as Mr Gladstone's Home Secretary, he was only 46. He exuded the 'effortless superiority' which was said to be the hallmark of the Balliol Man and he had established a fearsome reputation at the Bar, not least by his performance as junior counsel for Parnell in front of the Committee of Inquiry which examined the letters – all of them forgeries – which implicated the Irish leader in the Phoenix Park murders. He was also a mild imperialist – a qualification which meant that he attracted the support of

the Roseberyites and would, party managers felt, enable him to outflank the jingoists of the Tory Party. In fact only one obstacle stood in Asquith's way. He did not wish, at least at that juncture, to lead the Liberal Party.

Asquith's reason for declining to contest the leadership was rational but not romantic. The Liberal leadership was 'impossible ... without great and unjustifiable sacrifice of the interests of my family'. In short, he could not or would not afford to abandon his lucrative practice at the Bar. The prospect of leading a divided party into the long wilderness of opposition must have influenced his decision. The pendulum – a great feature of Victorian politics – was not expected to swing again for years. So he concluded that 'from every point of view ... the best choice our party could make [is] Campbell-Bannerman'.[5] *The Times* was sympathetic but hardly complimentary. 'If Sir Henry Campbell-Bannerman has a defect it is that he is not prone to excess of activity ... It is likely to be that he will turn out to be a warming pan from which neither light nor heat can be expected. Nevertheless, a warming pan has its uses'.[6] But in February 1899 CB became leader of the party in the House of Commons. He

'If Sir Henry Campbell-Bannerman has a defect it is that he is not prone to excess of activity ... It is likely to be that he will turn out to be a warming pan from which neither light nor heat can be expected. Nevertheless, a warming pan has its uses'

THE TIMES

told Lord Spencer, *I only fulfil that function with my commoners.* He was making clear that he did not expect to become Prime Minister. When the distant day of government arrived he was ready to step aside for either Spencer himself or a rejuvenated Rosebery to lead the country from the Lords.

As Leader of the Opposition, CB revealed previously unsuspected talents. Balfour, in the letter which (as Leader of the House of Commons) he sent each day to the Queen, described Campbell-Bannerman's first day as party leader with admirable generosity. 'His criticisms [of Lord Salisbury] at times were grossly unfair. But they were very well delivered and full of humorous touches and eloquent passages. It was a good beginning'. Morley agreed. Writing to Harcourt – who probably received the news with mixed feelings – he called the speech 'easy, amusing and a success as we knew it would be'. The *Manchester Guardian* thought it a 'sensation'. But it was neither the style nor the content which gave loyal Liberals most pleasure. It was the agility with which their new leader had managed to avoid committing himself to either the imperialist or radical wing of the party. Was it possible, they wondered, that the new man could unite the warring factions. The time was soon to come when all his powers of emollience and persuasion would be needed to avoid the Liberal Party destroying itself in a torment of bitterness and acrimony.

After CB was dead, Austen Chamberlain – who had inherited his apostate father's dislike of the Liberal Party – claimed that the new Leader of the Opposition was chosen by mistake. In December 1895, his allegation ran, Lord Tweedmouth travelled to Scotland with the intention of offering CB the succession purely out of courtesy. Service and seniority dictated that he should have first refusal but it was taken for granted that he would decline with thanks. His acceptance, Chamberlain said, was received with astonishment and profound apprehension. The meeting of Liberal MPs which confirmed his election in February 1899 did so – the story ends – with no enthusiasm and much resentment.

The story is almost certainly pure invention. With Asquith ruling himself out of the race, CB was the only alternative to Harcourt and the return of Rosebery. Both those propositions were anathema to the party. But it is true to say that virtually

no-one expected CB to be more than a bridging passage in the history of the Liberals and Liberalism. It was not only age – he was only 63 – and his health which colleagues held against him. In an era when Parliament was taken far more seriously than it is today, CB – before the end of the century – was an uninspired parliamentary performer. At his best, he was workmanlike. At his worst, he was unconvincing. His record was that of a competent administrator – not a virtue which always commends itself to politicians – and much of his administrative record was related to one department, the War Office. He neither attracted nor encouraged a faction of supporters. The one failed attempt to become Speaker aside, he did not push himself. And in politics it is people who push themselves who get on.

Finally, and perhaps most significantly, CB's manner and appearance were against him. At a time when the Liberal Party was looking for revivifying fire and brimstone, CB looked like, and behaved in the fashion of, a retired major general. In his most famous portrait – wearing the sash of a Knight of the Bath, the most military order of chivalry – it is easy to imagine that he had nobly served the Raj in India or commanded a brigade under Wolseley at Tel el Kebir. Politicians are often superficial people. The Liberals of 1899 did not realise that the old-fashioned moustache and the elaborately courteous manner hid a man of intellect and imagination. Like Clement Attlee – by whom he was much admired – CB came into his own when he became Prime Minister. During his brief premiership he made speeches which set pulses racing and took decisions which altered the history of the nation.

Chapter 5: The Resources of Civilisation

The Liberal Party's history had already confirmed that indecision over South Africa spelt ruination for the government. Gladstone had agreed on the annexation of the Transvaal, but had withdrawn all claim to the territory immediately after the Boers defeated the British army at the battle of Majuba Hill. However, the Matabele had been crushed and Cecil Rhodes was secure in Cape Colony – secure but not satisfied. His sense of mission was summed up in a single explanation of his conviction. 'I walked between earth and sky and when I looked down I said "This earth should be English" and when I looked up I said "England should rule the earth".' Others would have been satisfied with the Cape. But geology, rather than destiny, decreed otherwise.

Five years after the British defeat at Majuba Hill, gold was discovered at Witwatersrand in the Transvaal and Johannesburg, its capital, became the economic capital of the whole region. By the turn of the century, the annual national income of the Transvaal had risen from £196,000 to £4 million. Few Boers shared in the new prosperity. British immigrants made up two-thirds of the Transvaal's population. Some of them had emigrated directly from England and Scotland. Rather more had moved out of Cape Colony, attracted by the gold and the commerce which it brought. Paul Kruger, the Transvaal Prime Minister, rightly judged that the Uitlanders, as the newcomers were called, would soon be in a majority and told them openly, 'It is my country you want'. Kruger's resentment was increased by what he believed to be the Uitlanders' way of life. The Dutch Reformed Church, which dominated the Transvaal, prided itself on its rigid morality. The Uitlanders, on the other hand, encouraged 'luxury without order, sensual enjoyment without art, riches without refinement and display without dignity'. He wanted them to remain in the Transvaal for he knew that economic prosperity was dependent upon their experience and initiative, but he was not prepared for them to enjoy full civil rights. Encouraged by their failure to rise up in support of the Jameson Raid, he assumed that, as long as they earned a comfortable living, the Uitlanders would not object too strenuously at being relegated to the status of second-class citizens.

Three years of uneasy peace was punctuated by moments of both hope and alarm. The Transvaal signed a mutual defence pact with the neighbouring Orange Free State. Kruger offered a gradual revision of the Transvaal franchise, in return for a British declaration that Her Majesty's government renounced all claim to the Transvaal. Alfred Milner, the High Commissioner in the Cape Colony, turned down the offer out of hand and the rejection was endorsed, in more bellicose language, by Joseph Chamberlain, the Colonial Secretary. Lord Salisbury was confident that 'the country as well as the cabinet – excepting perhaps Mr Chamberlain – is against war'.[1] And even Chamberlain thought that war would not be necessary for the fulfilment of his imperial purpose. He accepted Milner's judgement that 'the Boers are still bluffing and will yield if the pressure is kept up'. Milner kept up the pressure on both the Boers and the British government. Invited by Chamberlain to summarise the situation in a public dispatch, he wrote 'the spectacle of British subjects kept permanently in the position of helots ... steadily undermines the influence and respect for the British government within the Queen's Dominion'. Chamberlain's response was probably bluff. He offered the Boers a choice between capitulation and war.

The Boers responded with an ultimatum of their own. No more British troops should be landed in any part of South Africa. A few desultory shots were fired in the direction of a British barracks. The Boers' effrontery changed public opinion. Asquith, who had denounced 'the irresponsible clamour which we heard, from a familiar quarter, for war', forgot how the escalating crisis had begun and demanded a strong British reaction to the Boers' ultimatum. The outcome was war – a result which he claimed was 'neither desired nor intended' but was forced on the government 'without adequate reason and against [its] will'.

The Leader of the Opposition had doubts about the wisdom of reacting with such vehemence to what he regarded as Boer posturing. Three days after the publication of Milner's 'helots' dispatch, he told a meeting at Ilford, *Some newspapers ... talk freely of the probability, and even the necessity, of war. I can see nothing in what has occurred to justify either warlike action or military preparation.*[2] *The Times* immediately accused him of increasing the dangers of war by encouraging the Boers to believe that Britain would yield to pressure and Joseph Chamberlain made a public offer in the House of Commons to give him 'on Privy Councillor terms' information which could not be disclosed in public. It was, and remains, a well-established technique for binding the Opposition to government policy. CB accepted the offer. Four years later, he made public Chamberlain's justification for sending a force of 10,000 men to the Cape. *The Right Honourable Gentleman went on to say 'You need not be alarmed. There will be no fighting.*

We know that those fellows – that was the Boers – won't fight. We are playing a game of bluff.[3]

CB was not quite convinced. He told the House that he *could see no ground for surprise at the stubborn resistance … to the proposal to admit Uitlanders to the franchise … Then there was the Jameson Raid … There is a certain strangeness in the idea that we should go to war to enable our fellow citizens to give up their citizenship in exchange for another*.[4]

He then went on a prolonged holiday – a decision interpreted by his friends as proof of his inner calm and by his enemies as evidence of his inability to rise to the level of great events.

The war began on 11 October 1899. Rosebery called for the nation to 'close its ranks and relegate party controversy to a more convenient season'. CB responded by announcing that the Opposition would not vote against 'supply' for the financing of the war. But his speech was sufficiently ambiguous about the merits of government policy to provoke Queen Victoria into writing in her journal, 'Sir Henry C Bannerman did not speak as patriotically as he should have done'.

Initially the war went badly for the British. They were vastly outnumbered – 10,000 horse and foot against 50,000 mounted infantry who knew the terrain. Lloyd George, who was unequivocally against the war, called it a contest between 'The British Army and Caernarvonshire'. In the early campaign, Caernarvonshire won. In one 'Black Week' there were defeats at Magersfontein, Stromberg and Colenso. In February 1900 there was a brief hope of quick success when the Boer commander Cronje surrendered. But for the rest of the year a stiffened Boer resistance taxed the army to the full extent of even its reinforced strength and forced the

War Office to replace the Commander-in-Chief. General Sir Redvers Buller was called home to make way for an older man. Field Marshal Lord Roberts VC, aged 68, assumed command.

Doubts about the moral justification of the war combined with the incompetence of its execution to persuade an increasing number of Liberals to ignore the balancing act – which the leadership was performing with obvious difficulty – and come down on the side of outright opposition. The young David Lloyd George was the most vehement of the government's critics. But John Morley was, in his patrician way, equally censorious. Rosebery, on the other hand, backed the war without reservation. He told a Liberal rally in Bath, 'I believe the party of Liberal Imperialism is destined to control the destinies of this country'. A distinct imperialist faction had begun to coalesce around him with – it was suspected – the covert support of Asquith.

The growing antagonism between the rival factions left Campbell-Bannerman with the choice of either splitting the party – by declaring that one of the alternative positions as the official Opposition attitude – or attempting to hold it together. He chose the

Field Marshal Lord Roberts ('Bobs') of Kandahar (1832–1914) won the Victoria Cross during the Indian Mutiny, and later commanded in Afghanistan. In 1880 he and his army conducted the celebrated 22-day march from Kabul to Kandahar (313 miles) to defeat the Afghan army under Ayub Khan. He was then Commander-in-Chief in India and Ireland, before taking over in South Africa. In 1901 he became the last Commander-in-Chief of the British Army (the position was abolished in 1904). Before the First World War he was prominent in the campaign to introduce conscription. He died of pneumonia in November 1914 on a visit to Indian troops serving in France.

second option, not least because he was suffering from all the doubts of a reasonable man. When, in November 1899, he read that Milner had admitted that Britain 'aimed at maintaining throughout South Africa the predominance of a single race' he denounced *the astounding and ill-omened words* as *not merely the departure from but the very antithesis of a sound policy*.[5] Having learned his lesson from his reaction to the Aldershot death of the two Highlanders, he went on to praise, in extravagant language, the heroism of the British troops. Despite the patriotic flourish with which his speech ended, the *Times* commented that the 'public has long watched with amusement the wobbling of Sir Henry Campbell-Bannerman'. It went on to record that he 'has come down from the fence at last ... On the wrong side and in pretty much of a heap'.[6]

His attempt to reassert neutrality – not so much between the Boers and British as between the warring factions of the Liberal Party – was doomed to failure. On one side Rosebery – supported increasingly in public by Asquith – endorsed government policy in the language of unapologetic imperialism. On the other the young David Lloyd George denounced, in equal measure, both the war and the Uitlanders it was being waged to protect. He claimed that 'the Kaffir workers of the Rand are better treated, have better wages and have more freedom under the domination of the "tyrant" Kruger than they enjoy in Kimberley or Matabeleland'. He accused the Uitlanders of 'lounging about in the hotels of Cape Town while English homes are being devastated on their behalf' and alleged that the whole British enterprise had been instigated on behalf of 'German Jews'. Sadly, he was not the only radical to appeal to the anti-Semitism which, at the turn of the century, was not very far below the surface of working-class jingoism. John Burns, soon to become the first working-class man to enter the Cabinet, Keir Hardie and even John

Morley all attributed the desire to control the gold mines of the Transvaal to the pressure of rapacious Jews. At least Lloyd George shared the blame between Israel and Birmingham. Joe Chamberlain, he said, treated the empire as if it was his own back yard and displayed the sign, 'No admission except on business'. He claimed that Chamberlain's imperialist instincts were reinforced by his family commercial interests. Lloyd George's tactics were summed up in the three emotive words 'Go for Joe'.

Throughout 1900 the split within the Liberal Party widened and deepened even as the British army appeared to be winning the war on the veldt. In June, Asquith wrote – with a cynicism which was only partially the camouflage of despair – 'I follow with languid interest the triumph of our arms and the dissolution of our party'. By the autumn the situation had deteriorated even further. When in October the government put down a motion endorsing the conduct of the war, Sir William Lawson moved a 'pro-Boer' amendment. He was supported by John Morley, Henry Labouchere, Lloyd George and 27 other Liberal MPs. Edward Grey – emerging as the Opposition's authority on foreign affairs – Asquith and 38 other members of the Opposition voted with the government. Campbell-Bannerman, the party leader, and 34 of his colleagues abstained – explaining that they were 'anti-Joe, not pro-Kruger'.

With the Opposition so hopelessly divided, and its leader obviously fearful of the accusation that he had befriended the enemy, the temptation to call an election was too strong for the Tories to resist. But the government's majority was only increased by four seats and the popular vote split 2,400,000 to 2,100,000. Indeed the results – described by Winston Churchill as a sign of the party's underlying strength – were so much better than expected that the imperialists began to fear for their position within the party. They decided to huddle together for warmth in what they called the Liberal Imperial Council. Its inaugural statement was intentionally offensive. 'The time has come when it is necessary to clearly and permanently distinguish Liberals in whose policies in regard to Imperial questions patriotic voters may justly repose confidence from those whose opinions naturally disqualify them from controlling the actions of an Imperial Parliament.' Campbell-Bannerman was so offended by the slur on his patriotism that, during a speech in Dundee, passion overcame precision. He referred to his critics not as Liberal Imperialists but Liberal Unionists. More sensitive about what was said about them than what they said about others, there were immediate complaints that CB had accused good Liberals of deserting the party and joining Balfour's Conservative coalition.

For a while the incipient Liberal civil war subsided into a co-ordinated attack on Joe Chamberlain. Then on 22 January 1901, the party conflict was stilled by an event which, although accepted as inevitable, still took the country by surprise and left it in a state of shock. After 60 years on the throne, Queen Victoria died at Osborne House on the Isle of Wight. Lord Roberts was back in England in time to lead her funeral procession. Three months earlier, he had been succeeded as Commander-in-Chief of the army in South Africa by Horatio Kitchener, his Chief of Staff. Kitchener continued Roberts' ferocious policy with even greater ferocity.

In February 1900, after his victory at Bloemfontein, Roberts had ordered that the farms which 'harboured men in league with the enemy' should be destroyed. Since Kruger's commandoes mostly consisted of 'irregulars', half the homes on the veldt could be classified as the refuge of Boer belligerents. When they were burned down, the women and children had to be provided with emergency accommodation by the British. Since the families were kept together in large numbers, they were said to be housed in 'concentration camps'. A new term entered the language.

The Boers, although beaten, would not surrender. So Kitchener devised a plan by which the veldt was cleared of the commandoes square mile by square mile. Barbed wire fences would divide the open countryside like a chess board and blockhouses would be built at the corners of the square. Each square would be systematically cleared of the entire population – farms burned and women and children taken to concentration camps. In June 1901, it seems that terror had won. Botha met Kruger at Middleburg and agreed that a truce was possible if an amnesty was offered to all 'Afrikaner rebels'. Milner told the Commander-in-Chief that he had exceeded his authority even by discussing a truce and that an amnesty was out of the question. Kitchener, stung by the rebuff, resumed the 'blockhouse and wire' strategy with renewed vigour. By June 1901 there were 60,000 men, women and children in the camps. The adult mortality rate was 117 per thousand and, among children, it was above 50 per cent. In the 20 months between January 1901 and February 1902, 20,000 detainees –denied medical supplies which were even scarce in the army sick bays – died.

Perhaps belatedly, CB had begun to set out a position on the war which was both distinctive and radical. It was the beginning of a new and decisive phase in his political life. In October 1901 he told the Oxford Eighty Club that imperial policy must be based on *conciliation and friendship, not domination and ascendancy – because the British power cannot ... rest securely unless it rests upon the willing consent of a sympathetic and contented people*. The new King was deeply offended by what he regarded as an attack on the government. Having yet to learn the limitations on a constitutional monarchy, he wrote to Lord Rosebery urging him to resume the Leadership of the Opposition. Rosebery had the wisdom to explain that the change which the King proposed was not possible.

The course of politics is often changed by small events and relatively humble people. And so it was with Liberal policy on South Africa. In December 1900 Emily Hobhouse – daughter of a Cornish clergyman – set sail for South Africa where she proposed to work for the Women and Children's Distress Fund. She visited the worst concentration camps and attempted to help the most distressed families. Women and children died in her presence. On her return to England Miss Hobhouse went to see Henry Campbell-Bannerman. Twenty years later she wrote, 'He left the abiding impression of a man who spared no time on pains to arrive at the truth and in whom wisdom and humanity were paramount'.[7] The meeting and the temperament which Miss Hobhouse described changed both Liberal policy and the Liberal leader's reputation. After CB's address to the National Reform Union at the Holborn Restaurant on 14 June 1901, the Opposition, although still not formally against the war, was unequivocally against the way in which the war was being fought. To the general public – and to King Edward VII – the distinction between the two positions was difficult to understand. The last words of the Holborn Restaurant speech have gone down in history. But, despite the resonance of those three sentences, other parts of CB's address have more content. What, he asked, is government policy in South Africa? His answer was a devastating indictment of 'blockhouse and wire'. Policy was, he said, *that now that we had got the men we had been fighting against down, we should punish them as severely as possible, devastate their country, burn their homes, break up the instruments of their agriculture ... It is that we should sweep ... as the Spaniards did in Cuba and how we denounced the Spaniards – the women and children into camps … in some of which the death rate has risen so high as 430 in the thousand.*

He went on to say that in the House of Commons he had asked Arthur Balfour for information about the concentration camps. His comment on the Prime Minister's response was the sensation of the year. *My request was refused. Mr Balfour treated us to a short disquisition on the nature of war. A phrase often used is 'war is war' but when one comes to ask about it one is told that no war is going on, that it is not war. When is a war not a war? When it is carried on by methods of barbarism in South Africa.*[8]

A phrase often used is 'war is war' but when one comes to ask about it one is told that no war is going on, that it is not war. When is a war not a war? When it is carried on by methods of barbarism in South Africa.

CAMPBELL-BANNERMAN

The predictable outcry was instantaneous. A clergyman wrote to tell him, 'You are a cad, a coward and a murderer. I hope that you will meet a traitor's and murderer's doom'. The *Morning Post* called CB's 'insults … as false as they were vexatious' and Rudyard Kipling ended several lines of doggerel with a slighting reference to 'the begger that kept cordite down'. Critics in the Liberal Party joined in the chorus of condemnation. Asquith wrote to his leader 'with more regret than surprise' and complained that the speech had been 'turned into an aggression demonstration by one section of the party'. Speaking at the Liverpool Street Hotel, he told the South Essex Liberals that 'a large number of colleagues in the House of Commons' wished him to say that 'we have not changed our view and do not repent it'. Dinner and denunciation followed dinner and denunciation in what came to be called 'war to the knife – and fork'.

Campbell-Bannerman thought it necessary to explain to

the House of Commons that he had meant no offence to the British Army. His explanation was not well received. Liberal Imperialists began to combine against him. Asquith, asked by CB not to attend a dinner which they had arranged, rejected the appeal on the spurious grounds that, having already accepted, it would be impolite to withdraw. And Lord Rosebery believed that he had found a perfect opportunity to vent his spleen on the Liberal grandees who had made his leadership unsustainable. During the summer of 1901, he opened a campaign which began with disassociation from CB's attitude to the South African War and was almost immediately widened into an outright denunciation of what the Liberal Opposition stood for.

His first salvo was fired after a lunch at which he had refused to make a formal speech. To general surprise, he suddenly launched into a demand that the Liberal Party 'start again with a clean slate as regards those cumbersome programmes with which [it was] overloaded in the past'. He then made a Delphic pronunciation about his own future. 'I must plough my furrow alone. That is my fate, agreeable or the reverse ... But before I get to the end of that furrow, it is possible that I shall not be alone.'

Fears that Rosebery was hell-bent on destruction were increased by a letter which he sent to the *Times* which described CB's attempt to unify the party as 'an organised conspiracy'. Then on 16 December his speech in Chesterfield left no doubt about the extent of his alienation. The time had come, he said, to abandon 'fly blown phylacteries' – an obscure metaphor built around the bundles of Hebrew text which Orthodox Jews wear as evidence of their piety. But there was nothing obscure about the assertion that 'he could have nothing further to do with Mr Gladstone's party' – not only because of its attitude towards the Boer War but equally on account of its policy towards Free Trade and Ireland. When he told the Chesterfield rally that 'the slate must be wiped clean' he was, in his strangely oblique way, demanding an end to the policy which had dominated Liberal politics since Mr Gladstone led the party – Home Rule.

The opposing armies in the Liberal civil war regrouped. The Liberal/Imperial Council was disbanded and replaced by the Liberal League – more moderate in its attitude to empire but more influential in that it could attract a wider level of support. Rosebery, still just a Liberal, became president. Asquith and Grey, his deputies, provided a greater threat to CB's leadership. Grey had become the party's acknowledged expert in foreign affairs and Asquith was in the invincible position of a man who knew that, had he so chosen, he could have been the Liberal leader. Rosebery's announcement that he meant 'to prevent his friends being drummed out of the party' made no sense. No-one was attempting such action. CB's only concern was for reconciliation. Asquith's declaration that he would 'have nothing to do with attempts to weaken or destroy the organisation of the party' was interpreted, not as a confirmation of his loyalty, but as a warning that he proposed to take over.

Grey openly sided with Rosebery in general and the Chesterfield speech in particular. But Lloyd George, speaking for Liberal radicals, told the *Pall Mall Gazette* that 'Campbell-Bannerman has enormously strengthened his hold upon the public during the last two years, especially in the last two months'. If that was so, the nation had begun to take to its political leader who consciously said very little and did nothing to increase his popularity. Six months before the war ended, he wrote to a constituent setting out the *three great enemies* which Britain had to fight to the death. *Devotion to material prosperity, national and individual*, like *apathy*, were anathema to all persons of a progressive disposition. But *love of sport and gambling in all forms* was rarely considered as a sin by politicians who hoped to lead their party to an election victory. Fortunately – for the country and for CB – the war ended on 31 May 1901.

The war had dominated British politics since it began before the end of the 19th century in the reign of Queen Victoria. But outside the House of Commons, men of conscience were beginning to consider domestic issues. Benjamin Seabohm Rowntree's second study of poverty in the city of York was published in 1901. Charles Booth's *Life and Labour of the People of London* was completed in 1903. It would be wrong to pretend that CB heeded the call to arms on behalf of Britain's poor. But he at least acknowledged the extent of the problem. Told that over 27 per cent of the total population and 43 per cent of wage earners lived below the poverty line, he would only express his astonishment that *a third of the people are on the verge of hunger.*

September 9, 1939

Part Two

THE LEADERSHIP

Chapter 6: 'Enough of This Tomfoolery'

By the spring of 1905, it was clear that the Balfour government was doomed. The Education Act of 1902 had alienated much Nonconformist opinion by promoting the extension of state schools which, in the view of Methodists in particular, would instruct pupils according to the canons of the Church of England. The Tory Party was bitterly divided between the faithful devotees of Free Trade and the proponents of at least some measure of protection. 'Imperial preference' was intended to cement the bones of empire while 'retaliatory tariffs' against countries which imposed customs duties on British goods were meant as rough international justice and proof that the Empire must be treated with respect.

As so often the case with a wounded government, unexpected crises increased the administration's peril. Enlightened opinion was scandalised by the government's apparent agreement to 'Chinese indentured labour' being imported into South Africa to work in the gold mines in conditions of near slavery and, what was worse, moral peril. The smell of office awakened Asquith's taste for leadership. Many Liberals, who had always thought of CB as a caretaker, looked for any candidate rather than the locum. Asquith was just one possibility. Spencer was favoured by the King. Rosebery clearly hoped for a return but was too conscious of his own grandeur to work in the hope of bringing the desired result about.

Grey told Asquith, 'You must be leader. Under no circumstances would I take office with CB as Prime Minister'.[1] Haldane thought Campbell-Bannerman a mediocrity who was not 'identified in the public mind with any new ideas because he has none'. In September 1905, he and Asquith visited Grey at Relugas in the Highlands where he was on a fishing holiday. Their initial inclination was to ask CB to accept a peerage and lead the Liberals in the House of Lords. But, having 'been made aware that this course will not be acceptable to certain sections of the party ... on policy even more than on personal grounds', they contented themselves with agreeing to insist that they should receive the key portfolios in the Liberal government which they anticipated would soon be formed – Asquith to the Treasury, Grey to the Foreign or Colonial Office and Haldane as Lord Chancellor.

However, Haldane, a natural intriguer, was not satisfied with what he regarded as half measures. In October he visited the King at Balmoral and was led to believe – or persuaded himself to imagine – that, if the Liberal Party won the election, His Majesty would suggest to Campbell-Bannerman that a younger man should be asked to bear the burdens of office. Whether or not the last hope of getting rid of CB was wishful thinking, it was soon frustrated. The conversation recorded in her diary by Mrs Asquith on 13 November 1905 marks the end of whatever chance there was of replacing CB. She was having her hair washed when she was interrupted by her excited, but not completely contented, husband who burst into the bedroom to report a conversation with Campbell-Bannerman. 'Suddenly he said that he thought things looked like coming to a head politically and that any day after parliament met we might expect a general election. He gathered that he would probably be the man the King sent for ... "What would you like? The Exchequer I suppose"'.[2] Campbell-Bannerman led

the Liberal Party into the election of 1905 because he simply ignored the intrigue of his colleagues and got on with the business of preparing for government.

Grey, less noble than history often suggests, and Haldane, even more arrogant than history usually records, continued to intrigue against their leader. The King was approached with the suggestion that, in the event of a Liberal victory, he should refuse to send for CB. The King declined to co-operate with the plan for two very good constitutional reasons. He did not want to risk the accusation that the court intrigued with dissident politicians in the manner of the Central European ruling houses, and he had come to like CB. In the years which immediately followed the Boer War, Edward had decided that his mother had been mistaken ever to think of CB as a steady hand at the tiller. The man was a dangerous radical. Then they met, by chance, at Marienbad and the King decided that he was a 'good fellow'.

As the election approached, Rosebery returned to the charge. At Bodmin, he was explicit in his opposition to Home Rule and, although critical of CB, more bitter about Liberals who shared his view but were afraid to speak out. He meant Asquith. But the putative Chancellor of the Exchequer, although a critic of what had been the Ark of the Covenant for 30 years, had come to an accommodation with CB. If Home Rule came at all, it would come step by step. Rosebery was not alone in his ignorance. Balfour chose to resign and force an election in the belief that, during the campaign, the Liberals would tear themselves to pieces. The decision to dissolve Parliament having been taken, he learned during a casual conversation with Asquith that unity had been restored.

Balfour resigned on 4 December 1905. There was some argument among the Liberal leadership about whether to form a government or force a general election. And there was a brief moment when the old hopes of dislodging CB were revived. But the prospect of power encouraged loyalty. Rosebery, who attempted to cause trouble during the campaign, only succeeded in alienating the Liberal rank-and-file from him rather than from Campbell-Bannerman. After CB made a promise that there would be no Home Rule until after a second election, the subject was barely mentioned. On 13 January 1906, polling began. The results, announced several days later, were a sensation. The Conservative Unionists won only 157 seats. Labour won 63 and the Irish Nationalists 83. The Liberals with 377 members had a majority of 132 over all other parties. Henry Campbell-Bannerman had presided over a landslide.

The Liberal triumph – now regarded as one of the turning-points in 20th-century history – did nothing to convince the critics that the party was led, and had been held together, by the right men. The rumblings went on. The King 'had a long interview with Sir H Campbell-Bannerman who undertook to form a government'. But the message from the Palace to the Prince of Wales cautioned with the news that 'nothing is settled and he has many difficulties in finding the right people'. Chief among the 'right people' who were causing difficulties was Grey who insisted that 'CB for some years has been out of touch with ... the most important movements of thought and action in the country'.[3] But his real reason for his reluctance to join a Campbell-Bannerman government was the loyalty, personal as well as political, he felt for Lord Rosebery – the man who had given him his 'first chance'.

CB – after consulting his wife and being reassured that her health, as well as his, would stand the strain – began to approach potential members of his Cabinet. Whatever Asquith said to the other Regulas conspirators, it is clear that after the triumph of 13 January he had no doubts about joining the government. After CB had sounded out both Lord Cromer and Lord Crewe and found each of them unwilling, he immediately approached Grey, through an intermediary, with the offer of the Foreign Office. Grey held out for a time. But with Asquith to support him, CB was always bound to win in the end. So Grey and Haldane agreed over dinner at the Café Royal that they had a public duty to swallow their objections and their pride and join the Cabinet as Foreign Secretary and Secretary of State for War. After that CB could get on with the routine business of forming a government. He did so with the official title of Prime Minister. All his predecessors as the head of government had constitutionally been no more than First Lord of the Treasury. Pitt, Gladstone and Disraeli had merely enjoyed a courtesy title. CB was, for the first time in history, the real thing.

At least one minister was grateful for CB's patronage. John Burns might have become Minister of Works, but the King objected to a man who had once been a republican taking responsibility for the upkeep of the Royal Palaces. So Burns became the President of the Local Government Board. When CB told him of his elevation, Burns replied with one of politics most memorable acceptance speeches. 'Well done, Sir 'Enery. That's the most popular thing you've done yet'.[4] It proved a disastrous appointment. When the Royal Commission on the Poor Law reported in 1909, it was Burns who, through indolence as much as prejudice, stood in the way of radical change.

'Well done, Sir 'Enery. That's the most popular thing you've done yet'.

JOHN BURNS ON HIS APPOINTMENT AS PRESIDENT OF THE LOCAL GOVERNMENT BOARD

Parliament met on 18 February – without the defeated Prime Minister. Balfour had lost his seat. He was returned as Member for the City of London in a swiftly arranged by-election and was back in the Commons on 12 March. It was the day on which F E Smith made what is generally regarded as the best maiden speech of all time and Lloyd George made his ministerial debut. But it was CB who, in Joe Chamberlain's metaphor, 'changed the weather'. After Balfour had intervened in the debate on Free Trade with a contrived speech full of irony, paradoxes, mock anguish and the same rhetorical devices with which he had dominated the Victorian Commons, CB lost his temper.

Enough of this tomfoolery. It might have answered very well in the last Parliament but it is altogether out of place in this.

CAMPBELL-BANNERMAN TO BALFOUR,
12 MARCH 1906

Balfour, he said, *comes back to this new House of Commons with the same airy graces, the same subtle dialectics and the same light and frivolous way of dealing with great questions ... Enough of this tomfoolery. It might have answered very well in the last Parliament but it is altogether out of place in this.*[5]

Henry Campbell-Bannerman's reputation was changed within the space of a four-minute speech. The boring stop-gap – who had been no more than tolerated by half of his own party and was supported only on sufferance until Asquith took over – had become the epitome of a new and more dynamic age. Balfour was the effete past. CB represented the radical future.

But the euphoria was not to last for long. As early as January 1906, guests at a reception which celebrated the election victory had noticed that the wife of the recently elected Prime Minister looked 'crushed with fatigue' and that when she called for a chair, her husband sat by her side – impervious of a host's obligation to his guests. There was talk that an 'excess of sugar in the blood' made her susceptible to every sort of disability from chronic depression to sudden physical collapse.

By Easter it was clear that Charlotte Campbell-Bannerman – who had long been an invalid – was mortally ill. In fact, she was a diabetic. And before the discovery of insulin there was no treatment for her condition. Ever since the discovery of Charlotte's illness, CB had chosen to be nurse and companion as well as husband. During the final weeks of her decline she would only eat when her husband fed her and demanded his constant presence in her sickroom. It was a terrible burden for the Prime Minister to bear. But he bore it without complaint. He did, however, feel a degree of guilt.

Three months after the Liberal government was elected, her condition deteriorated. She would allow no-one else to nurse her or to perform the domestic duties which were then expected of a Prime Minister's wife. Her demands were so great – and his determination to fulfil them so uncompromising – that in July 1906 he wrote to the King, *I have deeply felt for some time the neglect of my duty implied in my absence day after day. My wife however is so ill and weak that I cannot leave her for long. I am profoundly sensible it is not right.*[6] There is no way of knowing what the outcome would have been had Charlotte lingered. On 13 August 1906, CB took Charlotte to Marienbad, as he had taken her each summer for the previous ten years. It was a great relief for her. She hated Downing Street. But the burden on him increased. Arthur Ponsonby, his private secretary, recorded how the door into Charlotte's bedroom was always left open so that her husband could respond to her constant calls. The strain increased when the King arrived for his usual cure and expected his Prime Minister, with or without his wife, to pay court. Charlotte Campbell, as she wished to be called, died on 30 August. After a long and painful journey, CB buried his wife in the village cemetery at Belmont. She had made many demands – not all of them reasonable – on her husband. But he could not be reconciled to her loss. He faced the last great challenges of his premiership sick and alone.

Chapter 7: The Most Reckless Experiment

Foreign policy is conducted most successfully when the Prime Minister and Foreign Secretary work closely together. Campbell-Bannerman and Grey behaved towards each other – and the protection of Britain's national interest – with professionalism and propriety. But – partly because of earlier tensions and partly because of CB's detachment from foreign affairs – there was never the easy intimacy between the two men which would have enabled each of them to discharge their duties with complete success.

At least both men were united in the rejection of a popular clamour for an extended naval building programme which matched German expansion. The agitation went on for five years and climaxed during Asquith's premiership with the argument about building 'Dreadnoughts' which was typified by the popular clamour 'We Want Eight and We Won't Wait'. But, during CB's years in Number 10 – when an 'economist' as Prime Minister believed that he could at least postpone a massive warship building programme – the need to prepare for war should have become apparent. On 10 January 1906, the French Ambassador in London told Edward Grey that the intelligence service, which answered to the Quay d'Orsay, had learned that Count von Schlieffen, the German Chief of the General Staff, had urged the Kaiser to begin 'a fundamental clearing up of relations with France by a prompt war'. Perhaps

the government should have taken the warning seriously. Grey, who had some sympathy with the 'claustrophobic' position which Germany occupied between France and Slav Europe, certainly did not. Haldane cut £3 million from the Army Estimates. However, the Foreign Office emphasised in their telegrams to Paris that the Entente Cordial which had been negotiated by Lord Lansdowne and his French counterpart, Theophile Delcassé, in 1904, was still a major feature of British foreign policy. Not surprisingly, the Quay d'Orsay thought it necessary to investigate the practical consequences of the high sounding declaration. A handwritten note from Grey warned CB that 'the French Ambassador asked me today whether, in the event of an attack by Germany arising out of the Morocco difficulty, France could rely upon the armed support of England'.[1] The Morocco difficulty was Germany's claim that it was entitled to regard that country as within its sphere of influence. Kaiser Wilhelm had visited Tangiers and announced that all the powers had 'equal rights' in the Magreb and Mashrak. A conference at Algeciras was meant to find a peaceful solution.

When the Algeciras Conference convened, it was clear that only the representatives of the Austro-Hungarian Empire supported Germany's claim to influence in North Africa. But the French remained understandably anxious about the restless nation on their border. In the event of further German expansion in their sphere of influence, could they be sure of British support? Grey and CB agreed on a sympathetic but imprecise reply. But there followed, at first without the government's knowledge and then with its approval, discussion between the French High Command and the British General Staff. The result was an increasing, if implied rather than stated, commitment to what amounted to a mutual security pact of which most of the Cabinet knew nothing.

Kaiser Wilhelm II

The German Chancellor Otto von Bismarck had had his difficulties with William I, but he had always in the end kept control of policy in his own hands, thus assuring its consistency and coherence. None of William II's pre-war chancellors was capable of this kind of firmness. Count Leo von Caprivi (1890–4) and Prince Chlodwig zu Hohenlohe-Schillingsfürst (1894–1900) tried and failed, while Bernhard von Bülow (1900–09) was as Wilhelmine in style as the Emperor himself. To Bülow politics was a dramatic performance in which he had a leading role, and he delighted in the bombast and the artful posturings that imperialism and navalism made possible. His method of handling the emperor was to flatter him, which merely confirmed William in his worst habits... .

The assertion of control over the Emperor would have required a willingness on the part of Parliament to assume future responsibility for all aspects of policy. There is no indication that the members of the Reichstag wanted anything of the sort. This at least seems to be the lesson of an incident that occurred before the war.

In October 1908, the London *Daily Telegraph* printed an interview in which the Emperor had apparently made some gratuitously offensive statements about foreign powers, as well as claiming credit for devising the war plan used by the British in the Boer War. The British took this calmly, on the whole, but a violent storm of protest arose in Germany. There were demands for restraints on the Emperor's prerogatives in foreign affairs. Here, apparently, was an opportunity for the Reichstag to make some progress toward real parliamentary government. Yet nothing was done. As Theodor Eschenburg has written, 'the uncomprehending indignation and the tendency towards oratorical exaggeration that was characteristic of the whole Wilhelmine era, and the lack of any concrete political objective, caused the debate in the Reichstag ... . to blow itself out without result.' [Gordon A Craig, *Europe Since 1815* (Holt, Rinehart and Winston, New York: 1974) pp 258ff.]

The King was, however, told. Years later his Principal Private Secretary wrote that 'I am fully persuaded that C-B never apprehended the significance of the conversations with France nor did he see how we were being gradually committed. As a matter of fact, I doubt if Grey did either. [The French] with consummate skill were enmeshing the Foreign Secretary, pretending to him all the while that he was free'.[2] However, Grey himself, in his autobiography, wrote of CB's concern that the technical discussions might lead to a commitment, or at least an 'honourable understanding' that Britain would 'be reluctant to honour'. The degree to which they would be capable of meeting the obligation remained in doubt. Argument raged between 'Jackie' Fisher and Admiral Lord Charles Beresford about the type, as well as the number, of ships the navy needed – armament versus speed and firepower. The confusion, over aims as well as means, does not itself add much lustre to Grey's inflated reputation. It also confirms that CB, despite his interest in military matters, was basically detached from foreign policy.

But the Prime Minister was not prepared to limit the expression of his liberal instincts to domestic politics. Diplomacy – no less than any other aspect of the government's activity – was susceptible to sudden intervention by the Prime Minister. On his way to speak to a conference of the Inter-Parliamentary Union in Westminster he heard that the Russian Duma – the one vestige of democracy which the aristocrats of the Kremlin allowed – had been dissolved by the Tsar. He composed a new paragraph to add to his address. It concluded *La Douma [sic] est morte. Vive la Douma*. Handing the draft to his private secretary, he told him, *Rather too late, I think, to send over to the Foreign Office*. Confidence had combined with conviction to produce a refreshing expression of what the Prime Minister thought right rather than what the Foreign

Office judged to be convenient. He had no doubt about what he thought right for South Africa.

His view on the need for a generous settlement had been made clear back in 1902 – proving that opposition is not always as futile an exercise as it sometimes seems. When the war in South Africa was won and over and the peace negotiations began, the Boer leaders were reassured about the Conservative government's good intentions by Campbell-Bannerman's endorsement of the treaty which it proposed. It was, by any standards, a generous settlement. Both Dutch and English were to be regarded as the official language throughout the Cape and would be taught, with equal respect, in schools. The Boer commandoes (with the exception of those who were prosecuted for specific crimes) were pardoned and allowed to keep possession of sporting rifles. The British Treasury was to pay £3 million towards restocking the farms it had defiled. Self-government was promised for 1906. But suspicions ran deep. They were allayed by the discovery that the man who had condemned 'methods of barbarism' believed that the government would keep its word. Perhaps, even to his own surprise, it was Campbell-Bannerman who kept the final promise. His great achievement was the creation of a new South Africa.

The new government's first task was the removal of the stigma of indentured Chinese 'slave' labour. On the day after the general election result was declared, ministers decided that, although respect for contracts prevented the revocation of existing indentures, future recruitment would be immediately prohibited. Decency was thus satisfied. But it was not until four years later that the last Chinese miner left the Transvaal for home. Fortunately, in dealing with the long-term constitution of South Africa, CB reasserted his radical opinions.

Campbell-Bannerman had no doubt about what the new government's South Africa policy should be. At the height of the war, when the Boers were still registering victories over the British army, he had told a meeting in Glasgow, *Let us restore, as early as possible, and let us maintain those rights of self-government which give ... contentment and enjoyment to every colony which enjoys them.* He did not propose to change his mind as he moved from opposition to government. But he

Let us restore, as early as possible, and let us maintain those rights of self-government which give ... contentment and enjoyment to every colony which enjoys them.

CAMPBELL-BANNERMAN

was conscious that his plan for genuine reconciliation would be bitterly fought by both the Conservatives and his own Liberal-Imperialist colleagues. Lord Milner – whose administrative skills had done so much for South Africa before he became caught up in the clamour to subdue the Boers by force – regarded CB's position as 'insane'. When the Liberals won the general election, he judged 'the prospects very bleak owing to the ignorance and evil disposition of this wretched pro-Boer cabinet'. The Liberal majority was big enough to resist external aggression. But there were forces within the government – led by Haldane – which held much the same view.

Very limited progress had been made towards the achievement of the Vereeniging Treaty's promise of gradual evolution to self-government. The Orange River Colony remained subject to the Crown without any proposals for change. The Transvaal was offered what came to be called the Lyttleton Constitution. It amounted to little more than a legislature which was composed of partly elected and partly nominated members – with the executive appointed by the nominees. Even that highly limited step towards democracy was to be circumscribed by a governor's veto over new legislation. It was certainly not enough to satisfy CB. On the other hand, the Colonial Office argued for 'continuity'.

Campbell-Bannerman's radical instincts were confirmed – as was so often the case during his brief occupancy of 10 Downing Street – by what he regarded as a conclusive argument. It was provided by Emily Hobhouse who, without the author's permission, sent to the *Times* a letter she had received from Jan Christian Smuts. 'I sometimes ask myself whether South Africa will ever rise again'. She accused the English colonialists of regarding the country 'with unconcealed contempt – a black man's country good enough to make money or a name in but not good enough to be born to die in'. There is no doubt that CB agreed with much of what Smuts wrote. It was Smuts who came to London to argue South Africa's case for autonomy within the empire.

Much to CB's surprise, his arguments for awarding South Africa immediate Dominion status was supported within the Cabinet by Edward Grey. It was also enthusiastically endorsed by the Under-Secretary to the Colonies, Winston Churchill, who – since the Secretary of State was in the House of Lords – had the duty of presenting the government's position to the House of Commons. Smuts – appointed a member of the Imperial War Cabinet almost 40 years later – must have been astonished to learn that the Prime Minister who led Britain when it stood alone had always been sympathetic to CB's view that South Africa should govern itself. He recalled, years later, 'The first man I had to see was Winston ... I stated my case ... He said he had never heard anything so preposterous. England had conquered South Africa only three years before and here I was asking for my country back'.[3]

It seems that Winston Churchill – invited into the Cabinet, despite his lowly rank because of his role in the Commons

– changed direction when he saw the way in which the wind was blowing. And it was CB who decided its direction. Accounts of the crucial Cabinet meeting vary. But they all agree that, having decided what he regarded as right, the Prime Minister determined what the policy should be. Smuts wrote 'the man who wrought the miracle was Sir Henry Campbell-Bannerman'. Lloyd George recorded that the Prime Minister told his Cabinet, *I have made up my mind that we must scrap the Lyttleton constitution and start afresh and make partners of the Boers.* According to that account, the Cabinet 'decided in a few minutes to give the Boers responsible government'. Asquith — not altogether an unbiased judge – argues that 'the notion that CB was opposed in Cabinet or won it over in regard to the Transvaal settlement is a ridiculous fiction'. He attributed the new constitution to the assiduity of a Cabinet committee of which he was a key member. CB himself, in a letter to the King, was typically anodyne. *The desire of the cabinet was to introduce firstly responsible government into the colony at the earliest time. Examination and discussion however disclosed the fact that much information was lacking.*[4]

The truth about Campbell-Bannerman's role is probably revealed by a letter sent to him by Lloyd George (then President of the Board of Trade) on the day after the Cabinet had met. 'I hope you will not regard it as presumptuous if I congratulate you on the way you saved the government from disaster yesterday.' It seems that Elgin proposed a draft constitution which was little more than the Lyttleton proposals. It was on the point of acceptance when the Prime Minister urged colleagues to reject it in favour of a more generous solution – the details of which he did not specify. They were worked out in the committee, about which Asquith wrote when he ridiculed the idea that Campbell-Bannerman was the author of the South Africa settlement. The details were

Imperialism

John Atkinson Hobson (1858–1940) was a publicist belonging to the left wing of the British Liberal Party, a consistent opponent of imperialism and advocate of an active social policy which would make Liberalism attractive to the working class. His critique of British imperialism was in the tradition of English radicalism, which had always been sharply opposed to an aggressive foreign policy and was committed to the ideal of unrestricted free trade, not least on humanitarian grounds. In his book *Imperialism*, first published in 1902, Hobson denounced the jingoistic mood that prevailed in England at the outset of the Boer War, which he attributed mainly to unbridled propaganda by the press under the direction of capitalist interests. His chief aim was to preserve Liberalism from the effect of imperialist doctrine and pave the way for a consistent policy of social reforms. It is not accidental that the roots of his theory go back to studies of the problem of mass poverty in the great industrial cities in Britain... . 'Aggressive Imperialism, which costs the taxpayer so dear, which is of so little value to the manufacturer and trader, which is fraught with such grave incalculable peril to the citizen, is a source of great gain to the investor who cannot find at home the profitable use he seeks for his capital, and insists that his Government should help him to profitable and secure investments abroad.' In other words, modern imperialism was due to the acute competition of surplus capital which did not find profitable employment on the home market. This theory, which seemed self-evident in the case of the Boer War, was supported by certain key features of the British economic situation at the turn of the century. ... While the home economy showed clear signs of stagnation and the rise of the real wages had come practically to a standstill, Britain's overseas investments were shooting up dramatically. In 1880 the total investment abroad was about £2 billion, while by 1913 it had risen to almost double this amount – a substantial proportion of the nation's capital. [Wolfgang J Mommsen, *Theories of Imperialism* (translated by P S Falla) (University of Chicago Press, Chicago: 1980) pp 11ff.]

the responsibility of others. The historic shift in direction was the work of CB.

A committee of enquiry was sent to the Transvaal. While it deliberated, Parliament debated the idea of a self-governing South Africa. In the House of Lords, an embittered Lord Milner described Smuts' party as an 'insidious and absolutely consistent enemy of this country'. The King thought it right to add his own comments in a letter to the PM. 'After all the blood and treasure we have expended, it would be terrible indeed to hand the country over to the Boers.' Balfour attacked the government for abdicating its responsibilities as 'temporary guardians of the empire' and Rudyard Kipling wrote a doggerel verse (published in the *Evening Standard*) telling the dead soldiers of the Boer War 'Wake or your toil is in vain'. But the real bitterness was reserved for the House of Commons.

To his delight and astonishment, Winston Churchill – a mere Under-Secretary of State – was invited to open the debate on the proposals for the government. The choice was not made as the result of the Prime Minister's generosity or because the government Chief Whip had identified the signs of nascent greatness. Lady Campbell-Bannerman had become dangerously ill, and her husband preferred to stay with her rather than address the Commons. Constitutionally it was a strange affair. CB had no doubts that a South Africa (Revision of Constitution) Bill would be overwhelmingly defeated in the House of Lords. So the government proceeded under the fiction of the sovereign's Royal Prerogative. After an Order in Council was published, all that was needed to make it law was Commons approval of Letters Patent which stipulated the change of authority.

Balfour denounced the proposals in the most extreme language. They were, he said, 'the most reckless experiment ever tried in the development of colonial policy' and he predicted that the Transvaal would make 'every preparation, constitutionally, quietly, without external interference for a new war'. It was not clear against who the war would be fought. Only one Tory, F E Smith, supported the government in the vote which followed.

Winston Churchill, on the other hand, was a great success. His speech ended with an appeal for all-party support for the decision to 'invest the growth of a free constitution to the Transvaal'. Unanimity would change the nature of the offer. 'With all our majority, we can only make the gift of a party. They can make it the gift of England'. There was, however, one part of the speech which can only be excused by the fact that the world, and its moral standards, were very different in 1906. 'I come to the question of the natives. Under the Treaty of Vereeniging we undertook that no franchise should be extended to any persons who are not white men.' Balfour would have done better to predict the evil consequences of that provision rather than to condemn the whole proposal out of hand. At least Churchill had the foresight to add, 'We may regret that decision, but we are bound by the treaty'.

So the Transvaal became a self-governing colony and the Orange Free State achieved that status six months later and the road was opened for the creation of a federated South Africa within the empire which became the Commonwealth. That task was not accomplished until after CB was dead. But it remains his greatest achievement and one which the men who fought and won the battle with him insisted would not have come about without his leadership. In South Africa, freedom turned sour. Perhaps before the new constitution for the Transvaal was in place, CB began to worry about what lay ahead for the native South Africans. If government was particularly offended by the conduct of the government in Natal, according to Winston Churchill 'the hooligans of the empire' who were guilty of 'disgusting butchering of natives'. The Prime Minister himself asked Elgin, the Colonial Secretary, to give his support to the *long-suffering Zulus* and hoped that federation would *soon squash* the brutal regime in Natal. But he was a man of his time. The new South Africa constitution was, in 1906, the radical response to Britain's colonial dilemma.

Chapter 8: The Will of the People

The great Liberal landslide of 1906 also marked the emergence of the Labour Party as a significant force in politics. Within weeks of Parliament being opened, the three elements on its back benches – the Independent Labour Party (ILP), Labour Representative Committee (LRC) and Lancashire Miners – had come together to form the Parliamentary Labour Party (PLP). The main – in the opinion of some of its members, the only – purpose of the PLP's existence was the protection of trade union rights and interests. Membership of the Representative Committee had been hugely boosted by two legal judgements which prejudiced the unions' interests. 'Taff Vale' made trade unions responsible for both physical and commercial damage done to business and industry by their members in the prosecution of a strike, while the Osborne Judgement prohibited unions from contributing to the funds of a political party. It was assumed that the Liberal government, sympathetic to working men and their organisations, would redress the wrong.

John Burns urged the Cabinet to introduce a law which made trade unions free of all responsibility. CB expressed his personal sympathy for the proposal but the lawyers within the Cabinet – led by Asquith – would not agree. Instead, they drafted a bill which provided partial immunity. Ministers accepted the less radical alternative. However, before it could

be published, Walter Hudson, a LRC Member, introduced a Trade Disputes Bill which met the demands of the TUC and more clearly reflected the Prime Minister's personal view than the measure which was to be brought forward by the government. Hudson's Bill was remorselessly demolished by the Attorney General in a speech which was as brutal as it was analytical. But although demolished, it was not destroyed.

To the amazement of the House, halfway through the debate which followed, the Prime Minister indicated his wish to speak. *I have never been*, he said, *and I do not profess to be now, very intimately acquainted with the technicalities of the question, or with the legal points involved in it. The great objective ... is to place the two rival powers of capital and labour on equality so that a fight between them, so far as fight is necessary, should be at least a fair one.* He then went on, without consulting his colleagues, to advise the House to pass the bill which the Attorney General had declared unjust and unworkable. *I always vote on the Second Reading of a Bill with an understood reservation of details which are to be considered later. That is a universal practice. Shall I repeat that vote today? I do not see any reason under the sun why I should not.*[1]

The Prime Minister's only possible justification for behaving in such a way was the status of Hudson's Bill. It was Private Members' legislation. That notwithstanding, CB's conduct was greeted with amazement by the Commons and fury by those members of the Cabinet who had refused to support the Hudson proposals in the first place. Nevertheless, after heated discussion, CB's will prevailed. A government bill was introduced to give the trade unions complete immunity. But the series of constitutional innovations, which had begun with the Prime Minister arguing with his own Attorney General, continued. During the consideration of the Bill in a Committee of the Whole House, Asquith, the

Chancellor of the Exchequer, made a personal statement. He was, he explained, far from certain that the legislation which was being discussed was necessary or justified. Indeed, as a lawyer, he had profound doubts about its legal propriety. However, since the (possible unwarranted) benefits it offered were available to both masters and men, he was reluctantly willing to support it. So, to general astonishment, were the Tories. It was not, in Balfour's opinion, the time to antagonise the working classes. Nothing more clearly demonstrates that the age of the Common Man was about to dawn.

Naturally enough, CB's support for a full-blooded Trades Disputes Bill increased the esteem with which he was held both by the TUC and Labour Members of Parliament. But, equally inevitably, it damaged his reputation with the King. The King's Private Secretary sent the Prime Minister a message expressing the royal hope that 'the bill will not include a clause allowing what it rather absurdly called peaceful picketing, as if it could be ensured that any form of picketing could be free from occasional acts of violence and, at any rate, constant intimidation'. It was not the King's only complaint against his First Minister.

It was, in those more intimate days, the Prime Minister's duty to write to the King after every Cabinet meeting, describing what had taken place. It was as a result of these communications – written with wit and care – that Disraeli had ingratiated himself with Queen Victoria. CB was not of a similar inclination. The letters were, to him, a nuisance which diverted his attention from the serious business of government. For the start, his letters were brief. After a month or two they became terse. The King amended them with sarcastic messages of thanks for such a wealth of information. The court began to grumble on the King's behalf. Told by its principal private secretary that the Prime Minister was 'making an absolute fool of the King', Lord Esher – courtier and confidant to three sovereigns – replied that CB was 'too old not to be incorrigible'. He believed 'the indolence of age is upon him'. In a later letter to the King he elaborated the point. 'Viscount Esher believes ... that the Prime Minister has aged a great deal lately.... His disinclination to master troublesome policies has turned into impossibility... The work of the government even on large questions of policy like the education bill is carried on in the various departments without reference to the Prime Minister'.[2]

In fact CB was ill. The heart disease from which he had suffered all his adult life had grown increasingly serious with the passage of time. The annual visits to Marienbad, intended as a 'cure' under the supervision of a German specialist, had done little to slow the process of gradual deterioration. As a result, the Prime Minister husbanded his energy. Combined with the hours he spent with his increasingly dependent wife, the result of his caution was the appearance of indolence and neglect.

With or without the Prime Minister's personal supervision, the government filled its first year in office with a swathe of institutional reforms. As well as the trades disputes bill, legislation was introduced to regulate merchant shipping (always a cause of concern because of the owners' cavalier attitude towards safety and living conditions), to introduce a system of workmen's (injury) compensation, to prohibit plural voting and to alter the rules of school governance which had been set out in the 1902 Education Act. That act had, quite rightly, increased the number of state schools. In the growing 'maintained sector', religious instruction was required by law to be of a non-denominational character and that, according to the Nonconformists, amounted to the doctrine and liturgy of the Established Church. The consequent outrage, encouraged by the Liberal Methodists of Wales in general and Lloyd George in particular, had helped to ensure the Tories' defeat in 1906. Theology and political reality combined to guarantee that the new government would remove the Nonconformists' grievance. In fact they were frustrated in that endeavour by the House of Lords which – although it had gladly endorsed the revolutionary bill of 1902 – ignored both the government's clear mandate and the overwhelming vote of the House of Commons and rejected the measure outright. Their Lordships also refused to endorse the Plural Voting Bill. Both votes were the early shots in a conflict which was to develop into a full-scale war between Lords and Commons after CB was dead – and end with the Upper House being left with no more than the power to delay, rather than to destroy, legislation which had been passed by the Commons.

Despite the fervour of activity within Parliament, it is possible to argue that the real political highlight of 1906 was the decision by the Women's Suffrage Movement to intensify their campaigns after they had lost all hope of receiving the support of the new government. In October 1905, when a Liberal victory was no more than anticipated, they had chosen to test the Opposition's commitment to their cause by demanding its endorsement during a public meeting in the Manchester Free Trade Hall which was to be addressed by Edward Grey, the putative Foreign Secretary, and Winston Churchill, a recent Liberal recruit from the Conservative benches. Christobel Pankhurst – part of the mother and daughter trio which led the Movement – was in the audience with Annie Kenney, a factory worker from Oldham who had been virtually adopted by the Pankhursts. Churchill spoke first. As soon as he rose to his feet, Annie Kenny asked him if the Liberals would 'make women's suffrage a government measure'.

Churchill ignored the question. Kenney and Christobel Pankhurst began to chant. At the suggestion of the Chief Constable of Manchester, unaccountably in the audience, the question was written on a scrap of paper and passed up to the platform. When the request was ignored, they began to chant again. They were led into an ante-room where Christobel spat in the face of a policeman. When urged to 'act like a lady', she spat at the constable again and hit him on the side of the head. Both women were arrested, charged and fined. Annie told Christobel, 'We got what we wanted'. Christobel agreed. 'I wanted to assault a police officer.' The suffragists attacked those they thought should be their friends in the spirit of moral outrage. As a result, they lost support from the politicians and parties who, seeing life in more practical terms, resented being the victims of constant verbal and occasional physical assault – even in support of a cause with which they sympathised. Whatever CB's personal view, 'votes for women' was not a priority for the new Liberal government.

Immediately the new government was elected, the Pankhursts requested a meeting with the Prime Minister – less in the hope of obtaining his support than with the intention of exposing the Liberals' opposition to votes for women. They had already approached the Tory Party and believed – wrongly as it turned out – that Balfour was on their side. When the request for a meeting was rejected, a protest meeting was held in Downing Street. Suffragists forced entry into both the Prime Minister's official residence and his official motor car.

They were released, without charge, on the specific instructions of CB. The women were, he said, *seeking notoriety and would be successful if they appeared before a magistrate*. He did, however, agree to meet a delegation of what, by then, had become 'suffragettes'. Originally they had rejected the name which the *Daily Mirror* had invented with the intention of patronising what that newspaper regarded as a gaggle of silly women. But what began as a mark of derision became a badge of honour.

Campbell-Bannerman supported votes for women. He had abstained in the first suffrage vote in 1892, when Asquith and most of the 1906 Cabinet had voted against, and in 1904 he had made his personal position clear that he was *friendly enough to the cause*. However, he had responsibilities as party leader. To make his support public would be *at once elevated into a new pledge for the party*. It was not a *moment for new and rash pledges*.[3]

Emmeline Pankhurst (1858–1928) was the leading campaigner for women's suffrage before the First World War. She founded the Women's Social and Political Union in 1903, and after the Women's Enfranchisement Bill was talked out of Parliament in 1905, the campaign became increasingly militant and even violent, with arson, bombings and attacks on ministers. Emmeline and her daughter Christabel were arrested and imprisoned many times, but never gave up. The vote was given to women over 30 in 1917, and full equality in voting rights with men was achieved in March 1928, only three months before she died. (See *Life&Times: Pankhurst* by Jad Adams.)

The deputation which CB agreed to meet turned out to be larger than deputations usually are – 300 in all. Perhaps unwisely, he obeyed his usual rule of frankness. His personal view had not changed. *In his opinion they had made out, before the country, a conclusive and irrefutable case.* But his personal view was not what they sought or what he set out with admirable honesty. When *not expressing his own individual conviction but speaking (as he must) for others, he had only one thing to preach to them and that was the virtue of patience*. His advice – unusual for a Prime Minister to give – was *go on pestering*.

Only the moderated were satisfied. The Suffragettes were always more aggrieved by what they regarded as delinquent friends than they were enraged by out-and-out enemies. So the demonstrations continued. Then, in early 1907, the Suffragettes demonstrated outside Parliament. What began peacefully ended in violence. A number of women were arrested.

But the Commons had begun to stir. In March, a Private Member's Bill, extending the franchise, was debated in the Commons. The Prime Minister chose to speak during the second reading; *I am in favour of the general principle of the inclusion of women in the franchise ... a women pays taxes ... she has to obey laws ... in shaping which she has no share ... The stage is long past when it can be argued that woman, by her position in society, is sheltered in some mysterious way from the rough and tumble of life and is precluded from exercising a share in public affairs.*[4] In consequence, he would vote for the bill because *the exclusion of women from the franchise is neither expedient, justifiable or politically right*. The sentiment was more important than the syntax. The second reading vote was carried but the bill, being vulnerable private business, was talked out.

The King expressed his relief to the Prince of Wales. 'Thank heaven that those dreadful women have not been enfran-

I am in favour of the general principle of the inclusion of women in the franchise ... The stage is long past when it can be argued that woman, by her position in society, is sheltered in some mysterious way from the rough and tumble of life and is precluded from exercising a share in public affairs.

CAMPBELL-BANNERMAN

chised. It would have been far more dignified if the PM had not spoken on the Bill – or backed it up.' Then he thought it necessary to rebuke his Prime Minister. 'The conduct of those so-called suffragettes has really been so outrageous and done that cause (for which I have no sympathy) such harm that I cannot understand how the Prime Minister could speak in their favour.' The Prime Minister spoke in their favour because he believed their cause to be just.

Saying what he believed became Campbell-Bannerman's habit. And he invariably believed in the radical alternative. His genuine opinions burst out again when, after the refusal of the Lord Chamberlain's Office to licence Bernard Shaw's 'The Shewing-up of Blanco Posnet', a deputation of distinguished authors asked to meet him to discuss the subject of theatre censorship. The letter asking for a meeting was signed by Algernon Charles Swinburne, H G Wells, Thomas Hardy, George Meredith and James Barrie as well as Shaw himself. It complained that what amounted to the prohibition of a performance of Shaw's play was 'opposed to the spirit of the constitution, contrary to common justice and to common sense'. Campbell-Bannerman accepted the logic of the protestors' case and agreed to set up a Joint

Until theatre censorship was abolished by the 1968 Theatres Act, the Office of the Lord Chamberlain was responsible for licensing all plays to be performed on the public stage under the 1843 Theatres Act, which had confirmed the 1737 Licensing Act brought in by Walpole to silence his theatrical critics. Plays which were not passed by the Lord Chamberlain could only be performed as members-only club shows. This censorship was not just a matter of removing rude words and scenes of a sexual nature, however: for 200 years it effectively stifled all sexual, religious or political debate on the English stage.

Committee of Both Houses 'to inquire into the censorship of stage plays as constituted by the Theatre Act of 1843 ... and to report any alterations of the law and practice which may appear desirable'. His mistake was to make Herbert Samuel chairman. When the report was published, it recommended no change.

There is no doubt that CB was temperamentally inclined to take decisions and make statements without consulting colleagues – an unfortunate propensity which was increased by the attitude of his most senior colleagues. Asquith never ceased to be a rival. Haldane was arrogant, Morley remote. And Grey believed, almost as a matter of principle, that foreign affairs was nobody's business except the Foreign Secretary's. However, the real challenge to the government – to Campbell-Bannerman's authority and the supremacy of the democratically-expressed will of the people – came not from overseas but from one of the great elements of the British Constitution, the House of Lords.

The Liberal Party had been in formal conflict with the House of Lords since the peers had rejected Gladstone's second Home Rule Bill in 1893. Even Liberals who voted for the bill with reluctance resented the denial of democracy. Rosebery described the hereditary chamber in which he sat as 'a great national danger'. CB wrote that the Lords had *raised a wind which will not go down until their wings are clipped.*[5] In 1895, his election address was explicit. The undemocratic character and conduct of the Lords *can only be overcome by taking from the irresponsible Chamber the power of over-riding the representatives of the people.* In 1900 he had the chance, indeed the obligation, to turn his threat into decisive action. The occasion of the unsought confrontation was the Education Bill.

The debates in the Commons were enlivened by a reinvigorated Arthur Balfour – in a real sense the architect of the

1902 Act which the 1906 Bill was designed to amend. The government majority ensured that it concluded all its stages without major amputation. In the Lords, under the direction of Balfour – itself an affront to the Commons in which his amendments had been rejected – it was emasculated. The King and the bishops all supported the peers' behaviour. Radicals in the Cabinet – most notably Lloyd George – took the view that the Lords had to be first denounced and then defeated. CB believed that the President of the Board of Trade had gone too far and, after receiving complaints from the King, replied that *Lloyd George is essentially a fighting man and has not yet learned that once he gets inside an office his sword and spear should only be used on extreme occasions ... I greatly regret his outburst and hope that it will not be repeated.*[6]

> *Lloyd George is essentially a fighting man and has not yet learned that once he gets inside an office his sword and spear should only be used on extreme occasions.*
>
> CAMPBELL-BANNERMAN

Lloyd George neither repented not changed his ways. The King's private secretary wrote to the Prime Minister with the message, 'the King desires me to say that, notwithstanding your remonstrance, he sees that Mr Lloyd George has made another indecent attack on the House of Lords'. Notwithstanding Lloyd George's verbal violence and CB's constant attempts to persuade the bishops to see reason, the Bill – or, more properly described, a Bill – was returned to the House of Commons in a form which was barely recognisable as having its origins in the legislation to which the lower house of Parliament had given an overwhelming majority.

The Cabinet was not sure how to proceed. The damage done by challenging the Lords over Irish Home Rule was still fresh in ministers' memories. Everyone wanted to reduce the peers' powers. But there was no agreement on how it should be done. Mr Gladstone had fought the hereditary powers over Irish Home Rule and lost because the issue which the Commons had chosen to champion was unpopular with the people. Education, the advocates of caution argued, was a subject in which nobody, except the practitioners and the dwindling churches, was interested. The Cabinet concluded that, in the short term, the best course was to respond within the rules of parliament and simply refuse to accept the Lords' amendments.

When the amended bill was debated, Balfour 'spoke in the most defiant tones' but his performance did not match the mood of even his own backbenchers. Many Tories were apprehensive about the constitutional clash which they thought would follow and peers of all parties were desperately afraid that the only possible outcome of a major confrontation would be a reduction in their powers. Tory members of the House of Lords pressed Lord Lansdowne, their leader, to argue with Balfour in favour of concessions but concluded that the 'real difficulty lies in the fact that the Leader of the Party does not want a peaceable solution'. There were two days of negotiation – Tory peers in earnest conversation with Conservative MPs as well as the front benches of the two houses circling round each other. In the end, the peers decided not to surrender. They calculated that, in the country, the issue would be seen as Church versus Chapel, not Commons versus Lords, and that the Church would win. When the division came, the motion to retain the Lords' amendments was carried by 132 votes to 52. The Conservative Party was willing to antagonise Nonconformist opinion even though, when the Trades Disputes Bill had been debated, it had not dared to oppose trade union power.

During the speech in which he accepted that the Education Bill was dead, CB disproved the allegations – whispered by some of the Tory clergy – that he neither understood nor fully supported the changes which his government proposed. *Our aim is ... to secure a national not a denominational system, public and not sectarian, on the general basis of common Christianity instead of sectional Christianity.* He concluded with the rhetorical question which Balfour could not answer. *Is the General Election result to go for nothing?* and a peroration which echoed Mr Gladstone's promise to suppress Fenian violence. *The resources of the British Constitution are not wholly exhausted .... I say with conviction that a way must be found, a way will be found, by which the will of the people – expressed though their elected representatives, will be made to prevail.*[7]

The resources of the British Constitution are not wholly exhausted ... I say with conviction that a way must be found, a way will be found, by which the will of the people – expressed though their elected representatives, will be made to prevail.

CAMPBELL-BANNERMAN

It was, for Campbell-Bannerman, a rare oratorical triumph. The cause of his unusual success is clear. He believed, with deep conviction, in what he was saying. He had expressed identical views to Queen Victoria after the Lords had defeated Home Rule ten years earlier.

Lloyd George and Churchill – the two firebrands in the government – wanted immediate action to curb the power of the Lords. Most ministers, including CB, took a more cautious line. They decided to see how far the Lords would go. As anticipated, the Plural Voting Bill was rejected out of hand when it reached the Upper House. Other bills were prepared with no better intention of provoking Tory peers into continual abuse of their powers. The policy – called 'filling the cup(?)' – succeeded in so much as five government bills were lost. But public opinion remained stubbornly unmoved, even though CB toured the country to make a series of resounding speeches. *The present House of Commons was not elected to pass only such bills as commend themselves to the House of Lords ... We do not intend to be a government on sufferance or to act as caretakers in the House of a party which the country has rejected.*[8]

Chapter 9: The 'Still Unconquered Territory'

Although the government was clear about what it would not do, it was unable to decide what should be done. As is often the case when such dilemmas perplex ministers, a new Cabinet committee was created. It recommended that disputed legislation should be considered by a joint sitting of the two Houses – all the Commons augmented by 100 peers. CB dismissed the proposal as *too complicated*. Instead he proposed 'a suspensory veto' – an idea first suggested by Mill in 1836. Two days before he moved a resolution calling for that limitation to be made law, he suffered a minor heart attack. Nevertheless he opened the debate calling for a procedure which gave *effect to the will of the people as expressed by their elected representatives* and ensured that *within the limits of a single parliament, the final decision of the Commons shall prevail*. The motion was carried by a majority of 285.

So CB prepared the way for the great constitutional reforms of 1911 and set out the terms on which the battle – who shall rule, peers or people? – would be fought. And the occasion, as distinct from the cause, of that conflict arose during his final days in Downing Street. Asquith had been a cautious Chancellor of the Exchequer for the first two years of Liberal government. He had reduced the national debt by £45 million and kept the national accounts in permanent

surplus. Pressed by more radical colleagues to implement what they regarded as essential elements of domestic policy, he had refused to advance into what he called 'the still unconquered territory of social reform'. But where the calls of conscience failed, the demands of political expediency prevailed. The Liberal Party lost two by-elections which it was expected to win. The Labour candidate was returned for Jarrow, and Victor Grayson, the romantic and mysterious independent socialist, scored an unlikely victory in the Methodist Colne Valley. At the TUC Annual Conference in Bath, a resolution demanding the introduction of an old age pension was carried unanimously.

The government responded by deciding that it would indeed introduce an old age pension and that the scheme would be in operation by 1 January 1909 as the TUC had demanded. Its provisions would not, however, be as generous as the TUC had wished. Instead of being available to all men over the age of 60, it was to be made payable to men of 70 or more – assuming that they were not lunatics, vagrants or in receipt of an income of more than ten shillings a week. The rate would be five shillings for a single man and seven and sixpence for a pensioner couple.

The budget of 1908 was prepared in what can only be described as the golden twilight of Campbell-Bannerman's premiership. At last, and against all predictions, he had gained a mastery over the Commons – the result less of his powers of oratory than of the transparent demonstration that he meant what he said and said what he believed. He survived an honours scandal – peerages for party subscriptions – with his reputation more or less unscathed and skilfully negotiated his Presbyterian way thought the minefield of episcopal appointments. Charlotte was desperately missed but, the burden of being her constant nurse being lifted, he seemed to enjoy a new level of energy. He was even able to anticipate the government's future with a Cabinet reshuffle.

Ironically for a man of such conspicuous probity, CB's final days in Downing Street were clouded by accusations that the party which he led – though not the Prime Minister himself – had bartered peerages for party advantage. Mr James Smith of Stirling – a substantial contributor to the Stirling Burghs Labour Party funds – had been knighted. The inevitable allegation that he had been rewarded for services to the Liberal Party was rebutted with the counter claim that, like Othello, he had done much service to the nation. His achievements were said to include the production of a revolutionary rudder for the battleship HMS *King Edward VII* – a boast which was hard to sustain after a dismissed and disgruntled worker from his foundry first alleged, and then proved, that the casting had cracked and then been surreptitiously reunited by electric spot-welding.

The usual arbiters of honesty and honour then weighed in. A letter to the *Times* insisted that 'honours are bought and sold, the proceeds going to the war chests of the party in office'. G K Chesterton – speaking for the men and women who want a better world but are unsure what it is or where it could be found, announced to the general mystification of his readers that 'In modern politics … the mass of money is unimportant. Rich men pay into it and are made peers. Poor men are paid out of it and are made slaves'.[1] Both the Prime Minister and the Leader of the Opposition gave categorical assurances that they knew nothing of how their parties were financed, had never solicited gifts or loans and would not, in any circumstances, offer honours in receipt of favours. Nobody believed them.

> *'In modern politics … the mass of money is unimportant. Rich men pay into it and are made peers. Poor men are paid out of it and are made slaves.'*
>
> G K CHESTERTON

In fact, at least CB was innocent. Two years later, Herbert Gladstone, the son of the great Liberal leader whom CB had shrewdly made Chief Whip, confessed that he had raised money for the party. Indeed, he had made a profit on the 1906 general election by soliciting gifts of £275,000 for a campaign which only cost £100,000. However, 'in no single case did he even hint directly, or indirectly, at honours'. Where titles followed the elevation was coincidental. Everyone who had received a peerage or a knighthood during his period as 'patronage secretary' (the formal title of the Chief Whip) was a 'famous businessman' whose contribution to the strength and prosperity of the nation deserved recognition.

However, Winston Churchill – a conspicuously reckless politician – did not attempt a similar justification of his sortie into the honours system. While discharging his duty to reduce the number of Chinese indentured labourers working in South Africa, he had asked a mining magnate called Robinson to attempt working his mine with contract employees. 'In return,' Churchill told the Prime Minister, 'he asked me, if he did all this would the government be grateful to him and whether it would give him an honour.' The implied compact became public after CB's death and the unspoken bargain was not kept. In November 1910 the Permanent Secretary at the Colonial Office reported, 'J B Robinson has been to see me today in a really furious passion because he did not receive a baronetcy'.[2]

If CB's reputation was besmirched by these machinations, he redeemed it with his stubborn refusal to deny an earldom to Lord Curzon – whose service as Viceroy of India had been suddenly ended after a battle with Kitchener, the Commander-in-Chief, about who should have ultimate authority over the army. Curzon – who was out of favour with the Tory Party of which he was a member – had asked for an

earldom to accompany his resignation. He had then changed his mind. As an Irish peer he could sit in the House of Lords and that he proposed to do until he could not find a seat. The he changed his mind again. But the general election had also changed government. Pressed by the King to recommend the earldom that Curzon so wanted, CB was firm. He was normally happy to propose honours to political opponents, but Curzon raised issues of precedent and propriety. His own party had chosen not to reward him for his services in India. It would be quite wrong for their opponents to do so. Curzon was so angry that he stood against CB in the election for Rector of Glasgow University. CB won. It was his last victory.

On 13 November 1907, he spoke at a Liberal Party banquet at Bristol. It was the climax of a week of almost continuous activity – Cabinet, royal receptions, political rallies. The Bristol speech itself was preceded by a lunch at the Guildhall for the visiting Kaiser. Two major speeches in a day proved too much for a sick man of 71. Before the night was out he had suffered his third heart attack in a year. Rest was prescribed. He accepted the advice, but his holiday took the form of extensive, and demanding, travel – Paris, Biarritz, Bayonne and San Sebastian. He returned via Paris where he

Other 20th-century prime ministers have been involved in honours scandals. Lloyd George effectively sold titles to raise funds for political campaigning, through his 'agent' Maundy Gregory. This resulted in the passing of the Honours (Prevention of Abuses) Act in 1925, under which Gregory was prosecuted and gaoled in 1932. In 2006, allegations that the Labour Party had given peerages in return for 'loans' to the party, and that backers for the new academy schools had been promised honours, triggered a police investigation into alleged offences under the 1925 Act.

held a series of meetings with French politicians and was back in London for the opening of Parliament in early 1908. He did not attend the opening session. In February there was yet another heart attack. By March, Asquith was acting Prime Minister and everything was ready for the transition. Asquith told his wife that the King 'had quite made up his mind to send for me at once in the event of anything happening to CB …'.[3] Visitors found the Prime Minister white, drawn and speaking only with difficulty.

By the end of the month, the King was taking the change of Prime Minister for granted and had no doubt that it would not be long delayed. He wrote to CB to express 'the earnest hope that he will not think of resigning before Easter. Apart from any political considerations, the King feels sure that it would react injuriously on Sir Henry's health.'[4] The real reason was the royal hope of a Continental holiday and the firm intention not to return to Britain – no matter how adverse the publicity – if a new administration had to be formed. The Prime Minister began to prepare for the end – including making clear who should succeed him as Member for the Stirling Burghs. On 1 April 1908 he instructed that a telegram be sent to the King in Biarritz asking permission to resign office. The King agreed but refused to return home. Asquith travelled to Biarritz to kiss hands and receive his seals of office – sitting in the corner of a Pullman railway carriage with his deer-stalker pulled down over his eyes in the hope that he would not be recognised. At least he was able to persuade the King that the whole Cabinet should not follow him across Europe for their inaugural audiences with the monarch.

Asquith assumed office, but there was no question of CB being moved out of Downing Street. For three weeks there were periods of brief lucidity interspersed with long hours of

unconsciousness. Early on the morning of 22 April 1908, still in a coma, he suffered his last heart attack. He died at a quarter past nine. Asquith, who could have become the Liberal leader in his place and succeeded him as Prime Minister, spoke the first encomium in the House of Commons. 'He never put himself forward, yet no one had greater tenacity of purpose. He was the least cynical of mankind, but no one had a keener eye for the humour and ironies of the political situation. He was a strong party man, but he harboured no resentment. He was generous to a fault in appreciation of the work of others whether friends or foes. He met both good and evil fortune with the sure unclouded brow, the same unruffled temper, the same confidence in the justice and the righteousness of his cause.'[5]

Henry Campbell-Bannerman enjoyed a brief tenure of office. Much more was begun than was concluded. But his premiership marked a turning-point in political and parliamentary history. Under him and because of him, the government began to take responsibility for the welfare of the nation and accept that the colonial peoples had the right to self-determination. And, because the policies he pioneered were unacceptable to the hereditary establishment, his government made a curb on the powers of the House of Lords inevitable. He was a genuine radical and, equally important, he was a good man.

Part Three

THE LEGACY

Chapter 10: Conclusion

History judges prime ministers against two criteria – their personal qualities and the achievements of the administrations which they led. Henry Campbell-Bannerman's government was only a beginning. But it was the beginning of a revolution in British politics. After the proposals for an old age pension, incorporated in the Budget by Asquith in the months before CB died, there was a general acceptance that Whitehall and Westminster must take a direct and creative interest in the day-to-day welfare of the people. Balfour's 1902 Education Act had pushed politics in that direction. The Workmen's Compensation Act, passed during CB's first year in office, had continued the process. The Budget which Asquith introduced and Lloyd George carried through the Commons made the new view of politics permanent.

CB did more than enthusiastically endorse his government's social legislation. Political and social pressures might well have ensured that, even without him, the change in the government's role would have come about. But he presided over that great change. Mr Gladstone takes credit for the achievements of his first administration despite heartily disapproving of most of them. So CB is entitled to at least the acknowledgement that he supported what progress and pressure from the electorate required even doubting Liberals in his Cabinet to accept. The epoch-making peace with the

The Premiership

'With Sir Henry Campbell-Bannerman, I want the Palace of Westminster, the House of Commons especially, to act as the *grand inquest of the nation*', wrote the great constitutional historian Peter Hennessy about the division of power between legislature and the executive, between the Palace of Westminster and Number 10 Downing Street. 'I only wish that Sir Sidney Low, writing in 1904, had been committing to paper a description that held good for parliamentary life at any point in the twentieth century when he depicted the House of Commons "as the visible centre, the working motor of our constitution". I fear that Low and A V Dicey were more accurate when, with the development of the Cabinet in mind, plus the growth of the electorate and the rise of the party machine in the second half of the nineteenth century, they saw power by the turn into the twentieth as having seeped away from Parliament out to the electorate (when it came to the making and unmaking of governments) and up to the Cabinet (in terms of the initiation of legislation).' [Peter Hennessy, *The Hidden Wiring* (Victor Gollancz, London: 1995) p 141.] By 'up' Hennessy might as well have said 'up the road and turn left into Downing Street'. This is where the Cabinet meets, at the residence of the Prime Minister – or First Lord of the Treasury, as it says on the brass plate on the door of No 10. Campbell-Bannerman was the first person to be officially appointed as Prime Minister, all his predecessors being merely designated as First Lord of the Treasury. 'For all the accretions of functions and powers into what Campbell-Bannerman called *this rotten old barrack of a house,* the apparatus in No. 10 has remained a relatively slim machine, certainly compared with what is available to most heads of government.' [Peter Hennessy, *The Prime Minister* (Penguin Books, London: 2000) p 50] And Hennessy lists as the second most important function of the Prime Minister, after 'managing the relationship between the Monarch and the government', the power to decide who is in the Cabinet, 'the power to hire and fire ministers. [Hennessy, *The Prime Minister*, p 58.]

Boers was, on the other hand, an achievement for which he must receive the true laurels of personal success.

It is at least possible that, without his endorsement, the Treaty of Vereeniging would never have been signed. The defeated colonists were suspicious about the Tory government's real intentions. It was only when CB – who had rashly spoken out against the South African concentration camps – reassured them of Britain's good intentions that they felt sufficient confidence to endorse what was a generous peace settlement. What is beyond doubt is that, without CB's intervention, the creation of a South Africa Dominion would have been delayed for decades.

On the advice of the Colonial Office, most of the Liberal Cabinet was prepared to endorse 'continuity' – a small measure of self-government for the Transvaal and nothing for the rest. It was after CB's intervention that the whole plan was sent back to the sub-committee which had recommended the endorsement of the previous government's policy. The result was the tragedy of apartheid – imposed by the Boer minority whom CB had wanted to liberate. But the settlement set the pattern for the century. Until then the Dominion status on which the Commonwealth was built was regarded as suitable only for the English-speaking colonies – Canada, Australia and New Zealand. After the South African settlement it was gradually accepted that colonists who were neither Anglo-Saxons nor Celts were entitled to self-determination.

If, when measured by his government's achievements, CB's premiership marked the beginning of the new age, his personality was clearly more appropriate for what, even by 1900, was a fading view of how politicians should behave. He was the least flamboyant of men – apparently impervious to insult and wholly unaware of the need to ingratiate himself with press and public. He believed in doing his duty

as he saw it, and he was repelled by the idea of promoting his personal cause. He was neither 'quick' nor 'smart'. But he was both dependable and honest. He had very little 'side' but a great deal of 'bottom'. And, although he passed Tim Healey's test of 'being the sort of man you would go with on a tiger hunt', it is very unlikely that he would have ever set out on so pointless an enterprise.

Most important of all, he was a genuine radical. On each of the defining issues of the day he passed the progressive test. He supported women's suffrage, trade union rights, freedom from censorship and the great social reforms for which his successor took credit. He did so with the apparent certainty that common sense commended each reform. And that is the mark of the true radical – the certainty that the changes he proposed in society were reasonable as well as right.

And Sir Henry Campbell-Bannerman had one other quality which should commend him to history. His personal relationships – with his opponents, with his colleagues and, above all, with his wife – show him to have been a good man. That is not an attribute which, when judging politicians, history should overlook.

NOTES

Chapter 1: 'Out of a Tory Nest'

1. Augustine Birrell, *Things Past Redress* (Faber & Faber, London: 1937) p 242.
2. Quoted in John Wilson, *CB: A Life of Sir Henry Campbell-Bannerman* (Constable, London: 1973) p 42, hereafter Wilson.
3. Quoted in *The Western Mail*, 23 April 1908.
4. Quoted in Wilson, p 105.
5. J A Spender, *Life of the Right Hon. Sir Henry Campbell-Bannerman* (Hodder & Stoughton, London: 1923) Vol I p 62, hereafter Spender, *Life* I.
6. Spender, *Life* I, pp 41–2.
7. *The Times*, 16 March 1875.
8. Quoted in Wilson, p 59.
9. Quoted in Wilson, p 58.
10. T P O'Connor, *Sir Henry Campbell-Bannerman* (Hodder & Stoughton, London: 1908) pp 38–9.
11. Quoted in Wilson, p 59.

Chapter 2: An Excellent Administration

1. Quoted in Wilson, p 62.
2. Quoted in Wilson, p 63.
3. Quoted in Wilson, p 64.
4. Quoted in Wilson, p 75.
5. Quoted in Wilson, p 75.
6. Quoted in Wilson, p 78.
7. O'Connor, *Sir Henry Campbell-Bannerman*, p 24.
8. Quoted in Wilson, p 81.

Chapter 3: 'A Good Honest Scotchman at the War Office'

1. Quoted in Wilson, p 105.
2. Quoted in Wilson, p 192.
3. George Earl Buckle (ed), *The Letters of Queen Victoria* Third Series (John Murray, London: 1931) Vol II pp 512–13.
4. Quoted in Wilson, p 201.

Chapter 4: 'A Warming Pan Has its Uses'

1. *Annual Register* 1900 and 1901, quoted in Wilson, p 215.
2. Quoted in Wilson, p 270.
3. Quoted in Wilson, p 270.
4. *Annual Register* 1898, quoted in Wilson, p 282.
5. J A Spender and Cyril Asquith, *Life of Herbert Henry Asquith, Lord Oxford and Asquith* (Hutchinson, London: 1932) pp 120–1.
6. *The Times*, 17 January 1899.

Chapter 5: The Resources of Civilisation

1. Andrew Roberts, *Salisbury: Victorian Titan* (Phoenix, London: 2000) p 724.
2. *The Times*, 19 June 1899.
3. Quoted in Wilson, p 307.
4. *Annual Register* 1899, p 158, quoted in Wilson, p 309.
5. Quoted in Wilson, p 315.
6. *The Times*, 16 November 1899.
7. Quoted in Wilson, p 345.
8. Quoted in Wilson, p 349.

Chapter 6: 'Enough of this Tomfoolery'

1. Quoted in Wilson, p 424.

2. Quoted in Wilson, p 431.
3. Quoted in Wilson, p 445.
4. Quoted in Wilson, p 463.
5. *The Times*, 16 March 1906.
6. Quoted in Wilson, p 518.

Chapter 7: The Most Reckless Experiment
1. Quoted in Wilson, p 525.
2. Quoted in Wilson, pp 531–2.
3. Quoted in Wilson, p 479.
4. Quoted in Wilson, p 481.

Chapter 8: The Will of the People
1. *The Times*, 31 March 1906.
2. Quoted in Wilson, p 507.
3. Quoted in Wilson, p 510.
4. Quoted in Wilson, p 511.
5. Quoted in Wilson, p 549.
6. Quoted in Wilson, p 555.
7. *The Times*, 21 December 1906.
8. *The Times*, 10 May 1907.

Chapter 9: 'The Still Unconquered Territory'
1. Quoted in Wilson, p 580.
2. Quoted in Wilson, pp 582–3.
3. Spender and Asquith, *Life of Herbert Henry Asquith*, p 195.
4. Quoted in Wilson, p 623.
5. *The Times*, 28 April 1908.

CHRONOLOGY

Year	Premiership

1905   5 December: Sir Henry Campbell-Bannerman becomes Prime Minister. He is 69 years old.

1906   The Liberals win the election with a majority of 132 over all other parties, a figure that included their normal allies the Irish Nationalists and the Labour Party (Liberals: 377 Conservative Unionists: 157 Labour: 63).

Vereeniging Treaty. C-B overruled the caution of his Cabinet and secured complete self-governance for the two Boer states, Transvaal and the Orange River Colony.

Trade Disputes Act is passed, removing trade union liability for damage caused by strike action. The Act safeguarded unions against the precedent set by the Taff Vale Railway Company successfully suing the Amalgamated Society of Railway Servants after a strike in 1901.

The Women's Suffrage Movement intensify their campaign after it becomes clear that their aims will not be endorsed by the new government.

British ultimatum forces Turkey to cede Sinai Peninsula to Egypt.

Education (Provisions of Meals) Act – the 'Birrell Bill' set about appeasing the Nonconformists and offering the Catholic schools a loophole through the legislation, but was dropped by the government after amendments by the Lords. Local Authorities are allowed, but not forced, to provide free school meals to those in need.

Plural Voting Abolition Bill is rejected by the peers.

Merchant Shipping Act introduced regulations for minimum standards of food and accommodation on British registered ships.

History	Culture
Albert Einstein develops his Special Theory of Relativity	Oscar Wilde, *'De Profundis'*. Hermann Hesse, *Unterm Rad'*. E M Forster, *Where Angels Fear to Tread.* Strauss, *Salome*. Debussy, *La Mer*.
Armand Fallieres elected President of France. Joao Franco becomes Prime Minister of Spain. Edward VII of England and Kaiser Wilhelm II of Germany meet. In France, Dreyfus rehabilitated. Major earthquake in San Francisco USA kills over 1,000.	John Galsworthy, *A Man of Property*. O Henry, *The Four Million*. Foundation of *Everyman's Library* by Edward Dent. Andre Derain, *Port of London*. Massenet, *Ariane*. Invention of first jukebox.

Year	Premiership

1907   Colonial conference, the first to be summoned for business, rather than purely ceremonial purposes.

The Second Hague Conference. The 1899 conference resolution concerning the limitation of military expenditure is confirmed, with minor additions. The conference failed, however, to agree a general treaty of arbitration.

Britain and France agree on Siamese independence.

The Education (Administrative Provisions) Act introduced a school medical service that carried out medical examinations and minor treatments, the first personal health services to be established by Parliament.

Small Holdings Act for England improved the position of tenants and improved the opportunity for tenants to purchase land; saw the establishment of co-operatives of smallholders.

The Anglo-Russian Entente is agreed, resolving the interests of both countries in Persia, Afghanistan and Tibet.

New Zealand gains Dominion status within the British Empire.

Lloyd George Patents Act. Foreign companies were deterred from taking out patents simply to stifle competition from Britain.

Resolution on the House of Lords; moves to restrict the power of the House of Lords to veto legislation. Ignored by the Lords.

1908   Education Act – 'McKenna bill', a modified version of the 1906 Birrell bill, tried both to protect the Nonconformists and, to ease its passage through the Lords, appease the Bench of Bishops.

5 April: Campbell-Bannerman resigns, 17 days before his death, having served two years and 122 days as premier. He passed away at 10 Downing Street, the last Prime Minister to die 'on the premises'.

History	Culture
Edward VII in Rome, Paris and Marienbad, where he meets Russian Foreign Minister Izvolski. Rasputin gains influence at the court of Tsar Nicholas II. Peace Conference held in The Hague.	Joseph Conrad, *The Secret Agent*. Maxim Gorky, *Mother*. R M Rilke, *Neue Gedichte* First Cubist exhibition in Paris. Pablo Picasso, *Les Demoiselles D'Avignon*. Edvard Munch, *Amor and Psyche*. Frederick Delius, *A Village Romeo and Juliet*.
King Carlos I of Portugal and the Crown Prince assassinated. Manuel II becomes King.	Colette, *La Retraite Sentimentale*. E M Forster, *A Room with a View*. Kenneth Grahame, *The Wind in the Willows*. Anatole France, *Penguin Island*. Marc Chagall, *Nu Rouge*. Maurice de Vlaminck, *The Red Trees*. Bela Bartok, *String Quartet No.1*. Elgar, *Symphony No. 1 in A-Flat*.

FURTHER READING

Birrell, Augustine, *Things Past Redress* (Faber & Faber, London: 1937).

Churchill, R, *Winston S Churchill. The Young Statesman* (Heineman, London: 1967).

Dangerfield, G, *The Strange Death of Liberal England* (Harrison, New York: 1935).

Egremont, M, *A Life of Arthur James Balfour* (Weidenfeld & Nicolson, London: 1998).

Jenkins, Roy, *Asquith* (Collins, London: 1964).

—, *Churchill* (Macmillan, London: 2001).

Magnus, P, *King Edward VII* (John Murray, London: 1964).

Masterman, C E G, *The Condition of England* (Eyre Methuen, London: 1909).

O'Connor, T P, *Sir Henry Campbell-Bannerman* (Hodder & Stoughton, London: 1908).

Pugh, M, *The Pankhursts* (Allen Lane, London: 2001).

Roberts, Andrew, *Salisbury: Victorian Titan* (Phoenix, London: 2000).

Spender, J A, *Life of the Right Hon. Sir Henry Campbell-Bannerman* (Hodder & Stoughton, London: 1923).

—, and Cyril Asquith, *Life of Herbert Henry Asquith, Lord Oxford and Asquith* (Hutchinson, London: 1932).

Wilson, John, *CB: A Life of Sir Henry Campbell-Bannerman* (Constable, London: 1973).

PICTURE SOURCES

INDEX

A

Asquith, H H 2, 3, 10, 55,
56, 63, 66, 71, 74, 75,
76, 81, 82, 87, 88, 90,
91, 92, 96, 105, 110,
120, 125, 133, 136, 139
Asquith, Margot 55, 88
Attlee, Clement 68

B

Balfour, Arthur, 1, 7, 50,
53, 65, 77, 90, 92–3,
107, 120–1, 122, 123
Bannerman, Henry (uncle)
15, 24
Beresford, Charles 100
Birrell, Augustine 10
Bonar Law, Andrew 1
Broderick, St John 50–1,
54
Bruce, Colonel (brother-in-
law) 11
Bruce, Charlotte
see Charlotte
Campbell-Bannerman
Bryce, James 9
Buller, Sir Redvers 50, 54
Burns, John 3, 75, 92, 110

C

Cambridge, Duke of 7, 17,
19, 40, 45, 46, 48–9, 54
Campbell, Sir James (father)
11
Campbell, William (uncle)
10
Campbell-Bannerman,
Charlotte (wife) 10, 15,
34, 93–4, 107
Cardwell, Edward 16, 18,
21, 24, 25
Carnarvon, Earl of 38
Cavendish, Lord Frederic 33
Chamberlain, Austen 66
Chamberlain, Joseph 25,
37, 39, 42, 52, 53, 57,
59, 60, 70, 76, 77, 93
Childers, Hugh 22–3, 25,
30, 40
Churchill, Randolph 25
Churchill, Winston 76,
104–5, 107, 108–9,
115–16, 123, 129
Collings, Jesse 39
Connaught, Duke of 45, 46
Cowper, Lord 33
Crewe, Lord 92

Lowe, Robert 17

M
Marchand, Captain 63
Mill, John Stuart 11, 14–15
Milner, Alfred 70, 75, 78,
   103, 107
Morley, John 1, 27, 55, 56,
   61, 74, 76, 120

N
Northbrook, Lord 27, 30, 31

O
O'Connor, T P 22, 35
Oliphant, Laurence 11
O'Shea, Captain William
   33, 44

P
Pankhurst, Christobel
   115–17
Pankhurst, Emmeline 117
Parnell, Charles Stewart 14,
   33, 42–4, 63–4
Peel, Arthur 57
Ponsonby, Arthur 94

R
Reid, Wemyss 38
Rhodes, Cecil 57, 59, 60, 69
Roberts, Lord 45, 54, 74, 77
Robinson, J B 129

Rosebery, Lord 1, 47, 53,
   56, 57, 59, 60, 63, 66,
   75, 81, 82, 87, 90, 91

S
Salisbury, Lord 1, 37, 50,
   54, 55, 57, 58, 70–1
Samuel, Herbert 120
Sandhurst, Lord 19
Schlieffen, Count von 96
Shaw, Flora 59
Shaw, George Bernard 5,
   119
Smith, F E 93, 108
Smith, James 128
Smuts, Jan Christian 104,
   107
Spencer, Earl 33–4, 38, 65,
   87
Stead, W T 27, 30

T
Trevelyan, George 33
Tweedmouth, Lord 66

V
Victoria, Queen 5, 21, 40,
   72, 77, 113, 123

W
Wilhelm II, Kaiser 57, 98
Wolseley, Sir Garnet 25–7,
   31, 45, 54, 68

THE 20 BRITISH PRIME MINISTERS
OF THE 20TH CENTURY

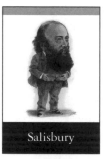
Salisbury

SALISBURY
Conservative politician, prime minister 1885–6, 1886–92 and 1895–1902, and the last to hold that office in the House of Lords.
by Eric Midwinter
Visiting Professor of Education at Exeter University
ISBN 1-904950-54-X (pb)

Balfour

BALFOUR
Balfour wrote that Britain favoured 'the establishment in Palestine of a national home for the Jewish people', the so-called 'Balfour Declaration'.
by Ewen Green
of Magdalen College Oxford
ISBN 1-904950-55-8 (pb)

Campbell-
Bannerman

CAMPBELL-BANNERMAN
Liberal Prime Minister, who started the battle with the Conservative-dominated House of Lords.
by Lord Hattersley
former Deputy Leader of the Labour Party and Cabinet member in Wilson and Callaghan's governments.
ISBN 1-904950-56-6 (pb)

Asquith

ASQUITH

His administration laid the foundation of Britain's welfare state, but he was plunged into a major power struggle with the House of Lords.

by Stephen Bates

a senior correspondent for the *Guardian.*

ISBN 1-904950-57-4 (pb)

Lloyd George

LLOYD GEORGE

By the end of 1916 there was discontent with Asquith's management of the war, and Lloyd George schemed secretly with the Conservatives in the coalition government to take his place.

by Hugh Purcell

television documentary maker.

ISBN 1-904950-58-2 (pb)

Bonar Law

BONAR LAW

In 1922 he was the moving spirit in the stormy meeting of Conservative MPs which ended the coalition, created the 1922 Committee and reinstated him as leader.

by Andrew Taylor

Professor of Politics at the University of Sheffield.

ISBN 1-904950-59-0 (pb)

Baldwin

BALDWIN

Baldwin's terms of office included two major political crises, the General Strike and the Abdication.

by Anne Perkins

a journalist, working mostly for the *Guardian*, as well as a historian of the British labour movement.

ISBN 1-904950-60-4 (pb)

MacDonald

Chamberlain

Churchill

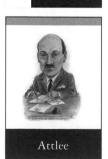

Attlee

MACDONALD

In 1900 he was the first secretary of the newly formed Labour Representation Committee (the original name for the Labour party). Four years later he became the first Labour prime minister.

by Kevin Morgan

who teaches government and politics at Manchester University.
ISBN 1-904950-61-2 (pb)

CHAMBERLAIN

His name will forever be linked to the policy of appeasement and the Munich agreement he reached with Hitler.

by Graham Macklin

manager of the research service at the National Archives.
ISBN 1-904950-62-0 (pb)

CHURCHILL

Perhaps the most determined and inspirational war leader in Britain's history.

by Chris Wrigley

who has written about David Lloyd George, Arthur Henderson and W E Gladstone.
ISBN 1-904950-63-9 (pb)

ATTLEE

His post-war government enacted a broad programme of socialist legislation in spite of conditions of austerity. His legacy: the National Health Service.

by David Howell

Professor of Politics at the University of York and an expert in Labour's history.
ISBN 1-904950-64-7 (pb)

Eden

EDEN
His premiership will forever be linked to the fateful Suez Crisis.

by Peter Wilby

former editor of the *New Statesman*.

ISBN 1-904950-65-5 (pb)

Macmillan

MACMILLAN
He repaired the rift between the USA and Britain created by Suez and secured for Britain co-operation on issues of nuclear defence, but entry into the EEC was vetoed by de Gaulle in 1963.

by Francis Beckett

author of BEVAN, published by Haus in 2004.

ISBN 1-904950-66-3 (pb)

Douglas-Home

DOUGLAS-HOME
Conservative politician and prime minister 1963-4, with a complex career between the two Houses of Parliament.

by David Dutton

who teaches History at Liverpool University.

ISBN 1-904950-67-1 (pb)

Wilson

WILSON
He held out the promise progress, of 'the Britain that is going to be forged in the white heat of this revolution'. The forced devaluation of the pound in 1967 frustrated the fulfilment of his promises.

by Paul Routledge

The *Daily Mirror's* chief political commentator.

ISBN 1-904950-68-X (pb)

Heath

HEATH

A passionate European, he succeeded during his premiership in effecting Britain's entry to the EC.

by Denis MacShane

Minister for Europe in Tony Blair's first government.

ISBN 1-904950-69-8 (pb)

Callaghan

CALLAGHAN

His term in office was dominated by industrial unrest, culminating in the 'Winter of Discontent'.

by Harry Conroy

When James Callaghan was Prime Minister, Conroy was the Labour Party's press officer in Scotland, and he is now editor of the Scottish *Catholic Observer.*

ISBN 1-904950-70-1 (pb)

Thatcher

THATCHER
Britain's first woman prime minister and the longest serving head of government in the 20th century (1979–90), but also the only one to be removed from office in peacetime by pressure from within her own party.
by Clare Beckett
teaches social policy at Bradford University.
ISBN 1-904950-71-X (pb)

Major

MAJOR
He enjoyed great popularity in his early months as prime minister, as he seemed more caring than his iron predecessor, but by the end of 1992 nothing seemed to go right.
by Robert Taylor
is Research Associate at the LSE's Centre for Economic Performance.
ISBN 1-904950-72-8 (pb)

Blair

BLAIR
He is therefore the last prime minister of the 20th century and one of the most controversial ones, being frequently accused of abandoning cabinet government and introducing a presidential style of leadership.
by Mick Temple
is a senior lecturer in Politics and Journalism at Staffordshire University.
ISBN 1-904950-73-6 (pb)

THE 20 BRITISH PRIME MINISTERS OF THE 20TH CENTURY

www.hauspublishing.co.uk